GENRE SCREENS from the Suntory Museum of Art

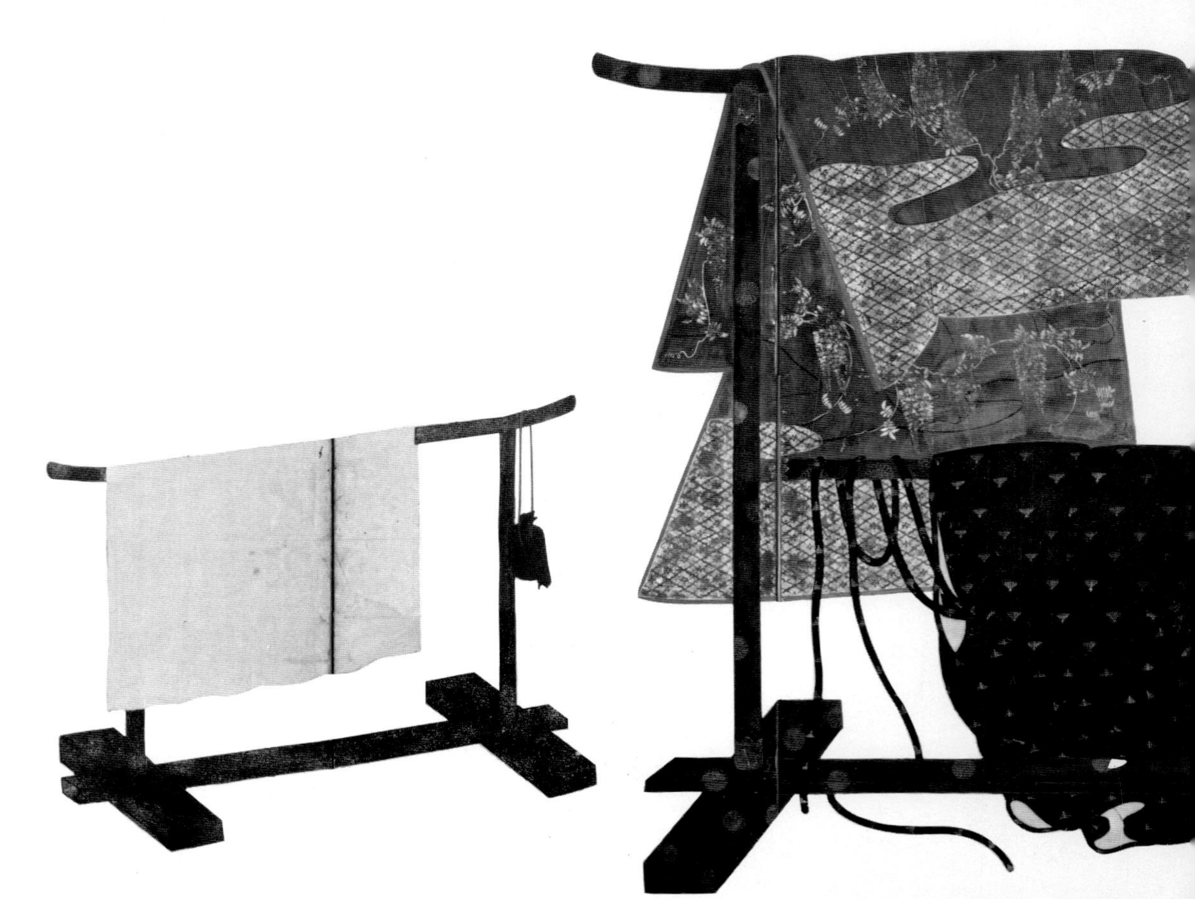

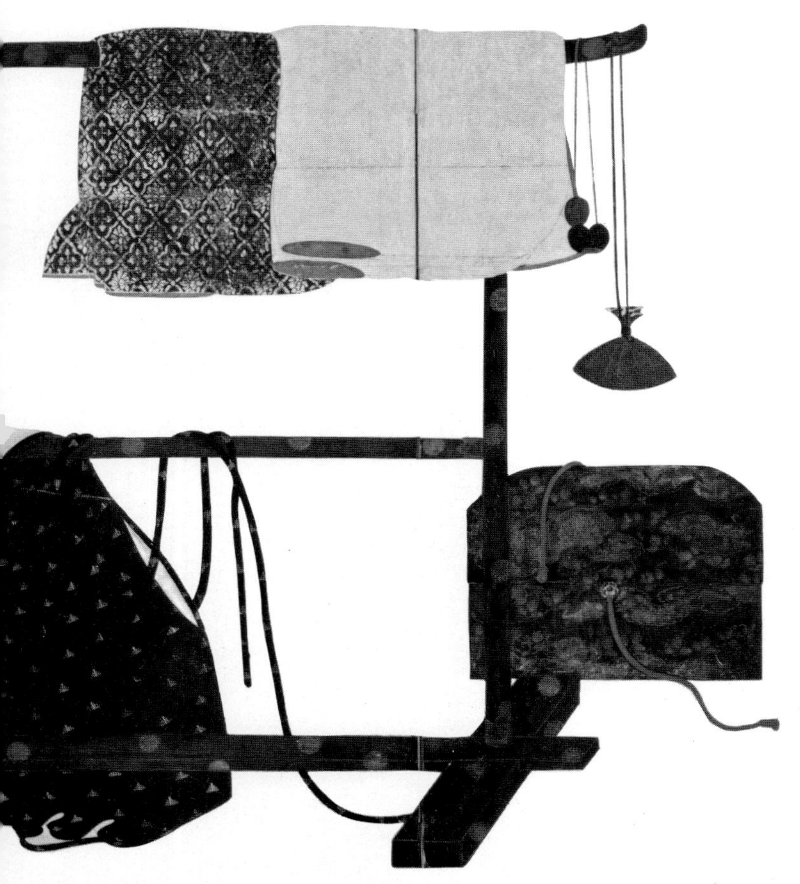

GENRE SCREENS from the Suntory Museum of Art

Okada Jō

Translated
by Emily J. Sano

Japan Society

The exhibition has been made possible in part by
a generous grant from Suntory, Ltd.

GENRE SCREENS
from the Suntory Museum of Art
is the catalogue of an exhibition of Japan House Gallery
shown in the spring of 1978 as an activity of
Japan Society, New York, New York.
Designed by Kiyoshi Kanai, New York, New York
Printed by Otsuka Kogeisha, Ltd., Tokyo, Japan
Set in Century Old Style and Franklin Gothic
by TypoGraphics Communications, New York, New York
The text paper is 135 gm. Toku Ryōmen Art
Photographs by Kojima Hirokazu, Tokyo, Japan

Printed in Japan
Library of Congress Catalogue Card Number 78-50644
ISBN 0-913304-09-3

Cover illustration: Catalogue 8
Entertainments at a House of Pleasure
Six-fold screen; color and gold on paper
Edo period (1615—1868), 94.6 cm. x 285.7 cm.

Contents

The Suntory Museum of Art, established in 1961, during the past seventeen years has built a collection of art objects created and refined by the Japanese over many centuries. The Museum has concentrated on collecting works that have been functional, useful objects in Japanese daily life, and the basic policy of the Museum is to give special attention to art and aesthetics in daily life. Further, the museum has held a large number of special exhibitions of varied content, showing works from its own collection as well as works borrowed from other collectors or institutions. These exhibitions have had the social character of Japanese art as their central theme.

While the folding screens in the present exhibition are works of art, they were also once used as furniture and functioned as dividers for large rooms. The pictures of famous places, depictions of shrine and temple festivals, and scenes of entertainments such as flower viewing and the Kabuki theatre painted on these screens demonstrate the rise of the power and dynamism of the common people in Japan, a phenomenon that dates to the sixteenth century. We value these paintings because they have preserved and transmitted to the present day an image of the ordinary Japanese of a former age. The Suntory Museum of Art is proud of the distinction that the Museum is the only institution which has this scale of holdings in this kind of genre screen painting.

It is our sincere wish that this exhibition will be viewed by large numbers of people in America, and that it will help to broaden their understanding of a people with a culture different from their own. On behalf of the Suntory Museum of Art I wish to express my deep appreciation to the Japan Society and the Japan House Gallery for their considerable efforts toward the realization of this exhibition and for the kind cooperation they have extended to us.

Saji Keizō
Chairman, Board of Directors
Suntory Museum of Art
President, Suntory Limited

Like frescoes from the walls of ancient houses, like stained glass from great cathedrals, the screens of the exhibition reveal clearly the interests, activities, and aspirations of the people of old Japan. We learn what amused them, what inspired them, and, as well, with what they clothed themselves and with what they surrounded themselves. No photograph could have better shown what Japan was from the sixteenth through the nineteenth centuries than these large, still, and very moving pictures.

Most of the material here is by anonymous artists. And the stylized figures, too, who people the pictures are anonymous. Painted to decorate the interiors of merchant houses or the palaces of lords, the screens served to brighten dark rooms and enliven social gatherings. The screens feature detailed representation of a variety of the daily activities of townsmen; festivals, dances, houses of pleasure—the special moments and places of a person's life—are but some of the themes included in genre painting of the time. The Suntory Museum of Art is especially rich in material of this kind, and the works gathered here well represent the Collection.

Screens, *byōbu,* were produced in Japan from earliest times and provided a large surface—usually, at least twenty-four running feet in length for each six-fold screen pair—which, with zig-zag folding, created one of the greatest challenges ever faced by painters. How well the Japanese met this medium is evident in the wide range of devices successfully employed in the screens presented here.

Screens had practical and architectural functions, too. They were made to be used as protection against breezes, divide rooms, and—in the use of expanses of gold—to reflect and extend the light of candles. Because they could be easily folded away, families might have several pairs on hand to be changed according to the needs of any occasion.

An international exhibition is always a complicated project, and many individuals have worked together to accomplish this one. Among them it is appropriate to express special thanks to Mr. Saji Keizō,* Chairman of the Board of Directors of the Suntory Museum of Art, and President of Suntory Limited, whose leadership in the organization of his company's museum and collection as well as his tireless efforts on behalf of this exhibition were critical to the success of this project. Mr. Okada Jō, long a friend of the Japan Society and distinguished champion of Japanese art, wrote this catalogue and selected the works of art included in the exhibition. His efforts were joined by associates at the Suntory Museum of Art, principally Mr. Hirai Senichi, Vice Director, and Mr. Yamaguchi Hisaichi, Chief Curator. Working with great enthusiasm the members of the staff of the Suntory Museum of Art guided us through the details of the exhibition with much skill.

Emily J. Sano, who translated the catalogue text, is owed much for her efficient and sensitive work on behalf of the exhibition. In addition to her duties as translator she undertook the responsibility of coordinating the development of the program in Japan. Working with her and the staff of the Suntory Museum of Art has been a pleasure.

Maryell Semal, Margot Kneeland, and Mitsuko Maekawa have been working with increasing devotion on every exhibition since the Gallery's inception. It is accurate to say the success of the exhibitions here is in no small way a result of their careful efforts. Kiyoshi Kanai and Cleo Nichols and their staffs again demonstrate in the graphic and installation designs a very high standard in the presentation of an exhibition.

May I also express here the sincere appreciation of all of us for the strong and continuing leadership of the Chairman of the Friends, Mrs. Douglas Auchincloss, and of the Chairman of the Advisory Committee on Arts, Mr. Porter A. McCray. The support of these two associations has made possible the Gallery program of bringing outstanding Japanese art to the United States for exhibition.

Rand Castile
Director
Japan House Gallery

*All Japanese proper names are given in Japanese style, family name first, given name last.

Translator's Preface

Emily J. Sano

Genre painting, a term that enjoys frequent use in the history of art, eludes easy definition. In Western art, as in Japanese art, genre painting refers to depictions of everyday life with the theme of manners, customs, labors, and recreational activities of anonymous people from all classes of society. While the concept of genre painting is firm in the West, the application of the term has varied, and its meaning shifted, depending on the age in which it was used and the type of painting to which it referred. Small scenes of everyday life existed in medieval art as part of larger works of a religious nature: for example, as small sections of stained glass windows or small scenes inserted into illuminated manuscripts. Generally, however, scenes of everyday life were not appropri ate subjects for painting until the work of Pieter Breughel in the sixteenth century and the Dutch masters of the seventeenth century. The genre painting produced at that time included landscapes, still lifes, animals and interiors, as well as scenes of everyday activities.

Genre painting in Japan coincides in time with its occurence in the West. Japanese genre began with the appearance of the Rakuchū-Rakugai (Scenes in and around Kyoto) screens in the early sixteenth century. These large paintings display the city of Kyoto and its many temples, shrines, residences, streets, and shops with a realistic, map-like accuracy. The city teems with figures, processions, and festivals that describe the various classes of society and detail their activities. The realism of Rakuchū-Rakugai screens inspired a rich body of related painting during the sixteenth century, and it encouraged the development of a number of interesting variations in the seventeenth century.

The character of genre painting changed gradually with time, and, in Japan, as in the West, genre painting is most easily understood when its separate categories of subject matter are described. Japanese scholars divide genre painting into as many as six to eight different groups. Famous places, ceremonies, entertainments, laborers, and depictions of ladies are basic categories, but others may be added to accommodate a particular point of view. The "Rakuchū-Rakugai" screens (No. 2) can be treated as a group separate from scenes of famous places, such as the "Higashiyama and Kitano" screens (No. 1), or "Itsukushima and Ama no Hashidate" screens (No. 4) in the present exhibition. Some sporting events, such as "Horse

Races at Kamo" (No. 14), can be placed in a category of festivals or in a category that focuses on the activities of warriors. The "Namban" (Southern Barbarians) screens (No. 17) that show the foreign merchants and missionaries who visited Japan in the sixteenth century, always comprise a separate category within Japanese genre painting, whereas, the "Tagasode" screens (No. 9) of folded kimono are sometimes counted as genre painting and sometimes not.

The artists who produced genre painting were not restricted to a specific school. Construction was at a high point in the sixteenth century, and artists were busy with commissions to decorate castles and residences. The Kanō school, whose artists combined brilliant color with the techniques of Chinese ink painting, was the most prominent group. The Kanō repertoire was diverse. They produced paintings of landscape, flowers and birds, historical and legendary figures, as well as genre. Artists of more traditional orientation such as those from the Tosa school, or those from the ateliers of independent artists such as Hasegawa Tōhaku (1539-1610) and Kaihō Yūshō (1533-1615) also produced genre paintings. A totally anonymous class of commercial artists called town painters (*machi-eshi*) worked as well to produce paintings for a steadily growing class of monied citizenry. Authorship had relatively little stylistic impact on genre paintings. Since most of these paintings are unsigned, it is now difficult to distinguish paintings by style or to establish their chronology with confidence.

Genre subjects were painted on fans, handscrolls, albums, and eventually hanging scrolls, but they were most popular for large surfaces such as walls, sliding doors, and the *byōbu* or folding screens. The folding screen had been an essential furnishing in Japanese residences for many centuries, and their broad, flat surfaces were used as a vehicle for painting from the Heian period (794-1185). Since a purpose of genre painting was to provide color and interior decoration, it is not surprising that the folding screen was the favored format.

The appearance of genre painting in Western art represents a significant departure in subject matter for artists, but even after the example of Breughel's realistic paintings, scenes of everyday life did not enjoy uniform acceptance throughout Europe. Nevertheless great artists produced genre painting—Vermeer, Caravaggio, and Le Nain, to name a few. Since they created works of undisputed artistic value, interest in these subjects endured.

The Japanese attitude towards daily life and the development of genre subjects was different from the Europeans. The depiction of customs and manners was an established part of paintings made during the Heian period. *Yamato-e,* a term that is used to distinguish paintings of native Japanese motif and subject matter from those of Chinese subject matter, is a traditional style of Japanese painting that developed during the Heian period. Famous scenic spots (*meisho-e*), activities appropriate to the twelve months of the year (*tsukinami-e*), and annual events of the year (*nenjū gyōji-e*) comprised the common corpus of *Yamato-e* painting. Japanese artists of the Heian period appear never to have questioned the suitability of their daily activities as subjects of painting. The study of Heian period *Yamato-e* is severely restricted today since so few paintings from that age are extant. However, scholars who have considered what survives and the literary records of the day are reluctant to label Heian art as "genre" because the common activities of people were not a central theme of these paintings. Although a Heian landscape may include a group of people on an outing, it is argued that the intent of the painting was lyrical, to show the beauty of nature in a particular season. The handscrolls of the late Heian and Kamakura (1185-1334) periods, such as the late twelfth century "*Shigisan Engi*" handscroll, or the thirteenth century biography of Priest Ippen, are full of genre elements, but the main purpose of the scrolls was narrative and not intentionally descriptive of daily life.

The genre painting that flourished in the sixteenth and seventeenth centuries was firmly grounded in the *Yamato-e* tradition. The Rakuchū-Rakugai screens present the city of Kyoto as a combination of landscape, religious sites, ceremonies, and events that come directly out of the Heian tradition. The many small scenes of Rakuchū-Rakugai painting, which individually could have decorated a fan, or appeared as a motif in a larger landscape, now appear in a unified composition that is no longer lyrical in intent, but descriptive. Moreover, Japanese artists were quick to apply these small sections of the city to independent screens, thereby making a single event or site the subject of a painting. Blowing up a single scene to large screen scale had the effect of making figures of people and their activities a theme of the painting.

Japanese genre painting differs from its *Yamato-e* foundation in scale and attitude. The large genre paintings displayed the activities of groups of people who were presented as types, not as individuals. The temples and shrines, scenic spots, and the events which had once been the theme of painting now operated as background. The artist was free to give expression to his interest in the common man. The reason for this new emphasis is frequently explained as a product of the historical and sociological events of the time. In the sixteenth century, after a long civil war, Japan was unified by a succession of warlords. That stability contributed to the growth of new towns and revived the economy. Celebrations were held; religious festivals were restored. The spirit of liberation and interest in life that permeated all classes of society led people out of doors to participate in outings and entertainments. Artists were attracted to this *joie de vivre.* People were active; they were colorful. For that reason they were made the subject of painting.

Japanese genre painting further departs from its traditional basis simply in the appearance of new subjects drawn from the contemporary scene. Theatrical entertainments, such as early Kabuki and its several variations, became popular subjects of painting as soon as they developed in the early seventeenth century. The dress and customs of foreigners (*Nambanjin*) who arrived in large ships were endlessly fascinating to the Japanese. The artists who recorded the labors of farmers and fishermen and the work of artisans and craftsmen gave their depiction full screen treatment. Conspicuous among the new forms of painting that developed in the seventeenth century are scenes of the gay quarters and paintings of women either in groups or as single figures. Isolated figures of beautifully costumed women evolved out of larger compositions as the artist narrowed his view from broad to gradually more focused scenes. Since an eye for color and decorative pattern is central to the Japanese aesthetic sense, these paintings can be appreciated purely for their composition and design. However, in a society so open about its pleasures, these ladies were intended to suggest something more earthy. The patrons of art now required of genre painting subjects that reflected more intimate personal desires.

In Japan the concept of genre loses its force after the seventeenth century. Individual artists, such as Hanabusa Itchō

(1652-1724) and his admirers continued to paint genre subjects
on screens. An example in this exhibition, "Taking Shelter from
the Rain" (No. 6) by Kō Sūkoku (1737-1811), is a painting of
anonymous people that copies an Itchō original. Furthermore, a
descriptive approach to subject matter survived the decline of
genre painting. "Sumida River" (No. 5) by Kuwagata Keisai
(1764-1824), an eight-fold screen which is unusual in this exhibition because it is executed in ink, describes a section of the
city of Edo famous for cherry blossoms. The Japanese love for
local scenery did not diminish but attention shifted from Kyoto
to the new capital, Edo. This screen is one of many produced
during the eighteenth and nineteenth centuries that perpetuated
an interest in the theme of famous places.

The attention of the public at large after the seventeenth century turned increasingly towards *ukiyo-e.* Japanese scholars
frequently state that *ukiyo-e,* the "art of the floating world"
commonly known to the West in woodblock prints, originated in
genre painting. From the foregoing summary it is possible to
conclude that those origins can be identified in new subjects of
painting that appeared in the late sixteenth and early seventeenth centuries such as the Kabuki theatre, the pleasure quarters, and depictions of women. Like genre painting, *ukiyo-e*
paintings and prints have subjects derived from a frank appraisal
of all the activities of the ordinary citizen. The spirit of immedi-
acy and responsiveness to life that characterized genre painting
continued to appeal to the common man. Just as genre painting
infused new life into the ancient *Yamato-e* tradition, *ukiyo-e* rein-
terpreted some genre subjects, retaining the motifs of the past
while discarding their sentiments. *Ukiyo-e* was an affirmation of
life. It was an art form that gave full expression to the social
complexities of the Edo period. By describing the color,
romance and dreams of ordinary people, it helped to confirm the
identity of the middle class. Genre painting of the sixteenth and
seventeenth centuries was therefore significant for having consolidated an attitude of openness toward general humanity with
realistic pictorial motifs.

Genre painting flourished in Japan during the Momoyama (1568-1615) and early part of the Edo (1615-1868) periods, an age that is often referred to as the "early modern" or *kinsei* period. Genre painting has as its theme the customs, entertainments, and activities of all classes of people. The rapid development of genre screens from the sixteenth century was dependent on a number of factors. The basis of genre painting is the tradition of "famous place pictures" *(meisho-e)* and "four seasons pictures" *(shiki-e)* of the Heian period (794-1185). *Meisho-e* and *shiki-e* were the subjects of *Yamato-e,* a purely Japanese style of painting decorating large surfaces such as the screens and sliding doors used in the residences of the nobility in the Heian period. These early decorative paintings show the scenery of various famous locales throughout the country and employ a variety of natural motifs and activities that were associated with the four seasons. Squares of decorated paper inscribed with *waka* poems appropriate to the scene were frequently pasted here and there on the paintings to create a combined pictorial and poetic aesthetic. Thus, when one looks at a painting of this type, the beauty of the location and season is made deeper by the sentiments described in the poem. The pictorial and poetic qualities of *Yamato-e* painting express the essential Japanese view of nature which is to blend and unify the natural world with human beings.

The native *Yamato-e* aesthetic remained a basic tradition in painting throughout the centuries in Japan. However, from the sixteenth century the focus in painting was more on people than on nature, and particularly in the outward appearance of people rather than their feelings. By the second half of the sixteenth century the end of a long period of warfare was marked by a lively spirit of frankness. All classes of people enjoyed outdoor entertainments together; festivals and ceremonies were revived, and a boldness in dress became fashionable. The rise of genre painting at this time is also directly related to the construction, on a large scale, of residences for the warrior class in an architectural style called *shoin zukuri.* Residences in this style are characterized by having a principal room that features a bay window with a low ledge before it that can be used as a writing desk *(shoin)*, an alcove with irregular shelves *(chigai-dana)*, and a recessed wall space for displaying paintings *(toko-noma)*. The need for decorating the wall and door surfaces in residences resulted in an increase in the demand for screens. Artists devised new subjects of painting, and their work is characterized by bold effects achieved through a lavish use of color and gold on large surfaces. Genre screens were not the exclusive possession of the warrior elite. The townsfolk of Kyoto and other cities grew in economic power during the Momoyama and early Edo periods. As this class of merchant and tradesmen acquired the means to become the patrons of culture, they too ordered screens.

Genre painting, especially genre painting on screens, changed slowly with the passing of the "early modern" age. Because the number of screens in this exhibition is limited, this essay does not attempt to pursue the elements of their historical or stylistic development, but simply to demonstrate the variety of subject matter included in genre screens.

The screens in this exhibition have been divided into five categories:
1. *Famous Places*
2. *Pleasures*
3. *Festivals*
4. *Common People*
5. *Namban*

Famous Places paintings have subjects based on the same native themes of "famous place pictures" *(meisho-e)* and "four seasons pictures" *(shiki-e)* of traditional Heian period painting, but the lyricism typical of Heian art is overshadowed in the sixteenth and seventeenth centuries by a modern realism that permeates the paintings. Numerous examples of this category of Famous Places paintings are extant, but the most representative type is the "Rakuchū-Rakugai" screen (No. 2) which makes its subject matter the city of Kyoto and its environs. The first Rakuchū-Rakugai screens were made at the beginning of the sixteenth century, and they were very popular for at least a century. These screens were commissioned by military lords to take to their home provinces as souvenirs, or by wealthy merchants to give away as presents. Another screen in this exhibition that makes Kyoto its subject matter is the one called "Higashiyama and Kitano" (No. 1); however, unlike the panoramic view of the "Rakuchū-Rakugai" screens, the scene is limited to a few shrines and temples.

"Celebrated Places in Ōmi Province" (No. 3) and "Itsuku-shima and Ama no Hashidate" (No. 4), on the other hand, both depict traditionally famous scenic spots. The "Sumida River" screen (No. 5) takes as its subject matter a section of that river in Edo City, or modern Tokyo, that was famous for its cherry trees.

Scenes of pleasure are a subject matter that best typify the genre painting of the Momoyama and early Edo periods. Among these are two basic types: those showing pleasures outdoors, "Merrymaking under the Cherry Blossoms" (No. 6), and the type that shows entertainments, games and music, indoors. Of the latter type, two are included in this exhibition, "New Year's Amusements" (No. 7) and "Entertainments at a House of Plea-sure" (No. 8). The "Tagasode" screen (No. 9), which displays the beauty of kimono decoration, is a motif known through numerous extant examples. The "Tagasode" screen could be considered a separate group in itself, but because the pleasure of looking at a kimono can be considered an indoor pleasure, it is placed in this category. Scenes of the Kabuki theatre were favorite subjects of genre painting, and these, too, can stand as a group by themselves, However, if one takes the point of view that Kabuki and flower viewing are objects of entertainment, it is appropriate to place the "Okuni Kabuki" screen (No. 10) and the "Flower Viewing at Ueno and a Kabuki Theatre" pair (No. 11) into the Pleasures category.

The festivals that were held at important temples and shrines, and various public events popular among the nobil-ity and warriors, became favorite subjects of painting. Exam-ples of this Festivals category included in the exhibition are the "Festivals of Shitennō-ji and Sumiyoshi Shrine" (No. 12), the "Archery Contest at Sanjūsangen-dō" (No. 13), and "Horse Races at Kamo" (No. 14).

Since the subject of genre painting includes most human activities, the lives of the common people are an appropriate subject. Screens that depict various craftsmen and laborers at work were numerous in Japan's "early modern" period. A com-mon type of painting in this category was the "cultivation pic-ture" (*kōsaku-zu*) which focused on agrarian activities. The "Fishery Scenes" screens (No. 15), which make fishermen the primary subject matter, fall into this "cultivation picture" cate-gory, but this particular variation is very rare. The nineteenth century screen of "Taking Shelter from the Rain" (No. 16), which is also placed in the Common People category, is a depic-tion of a group of working people brought together by chance during a storm. Here the artist captures the spirit of common people rather than the specific activities of the individuals of this group as seen in other screens, such as "Fishery Scenes."

The "Namban Screen" (No. 17) brings to genre painting the appearance, manners, and customs of the so-called "Southern Barbarians" (*Nambanjin*), the Portuguese merchants and missionaries who came to Japan on ships at the beginning of the sixteenth century. A number of screens with this subject matter exist, and they are all very similar in style.

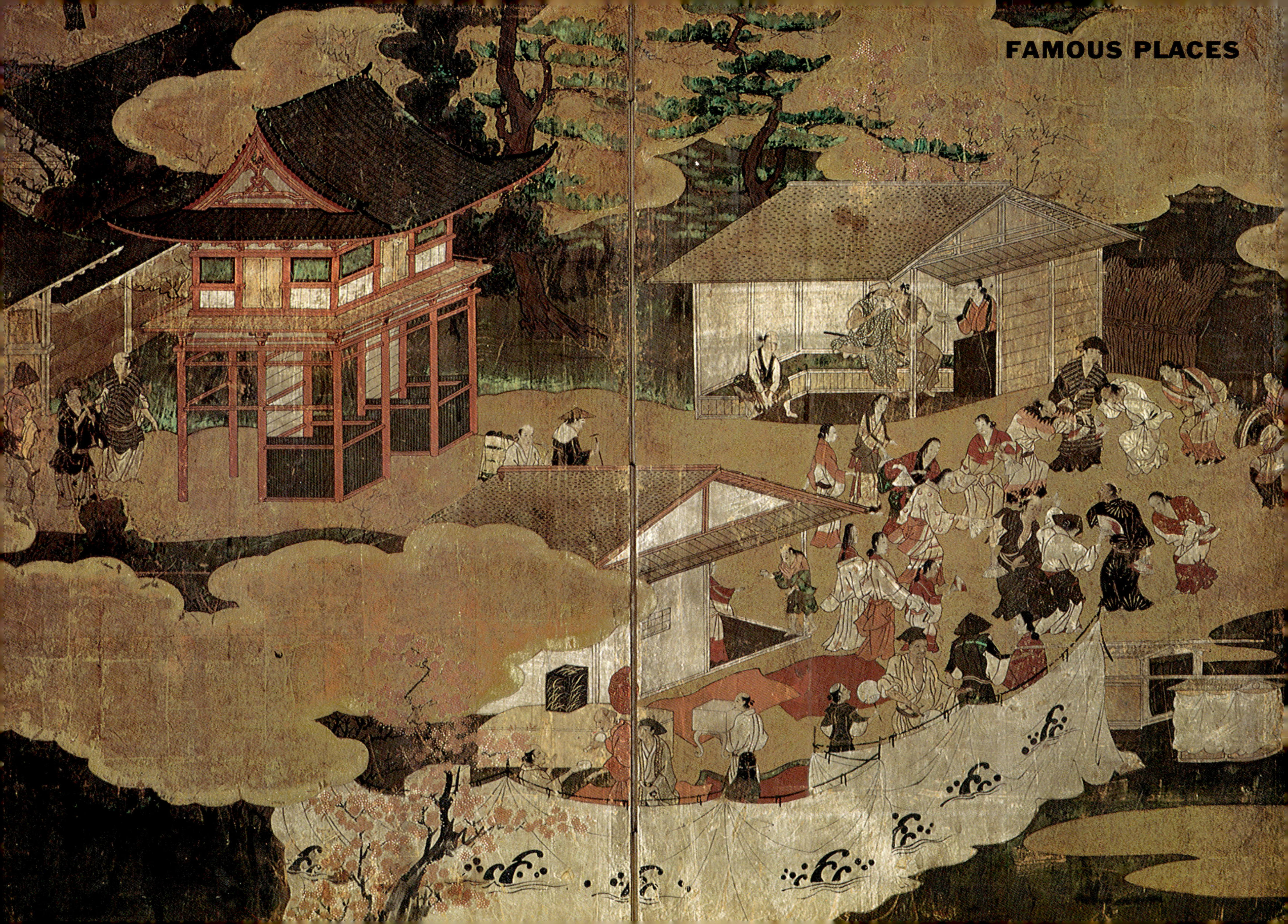
FAMOUS PLACES

1.
HIGASHIYAMA AND KITANO
Momoyama period, seventeenth century
Pair of six-fold screens; color and gold on paper
168.5 cm. x 349 cm., each

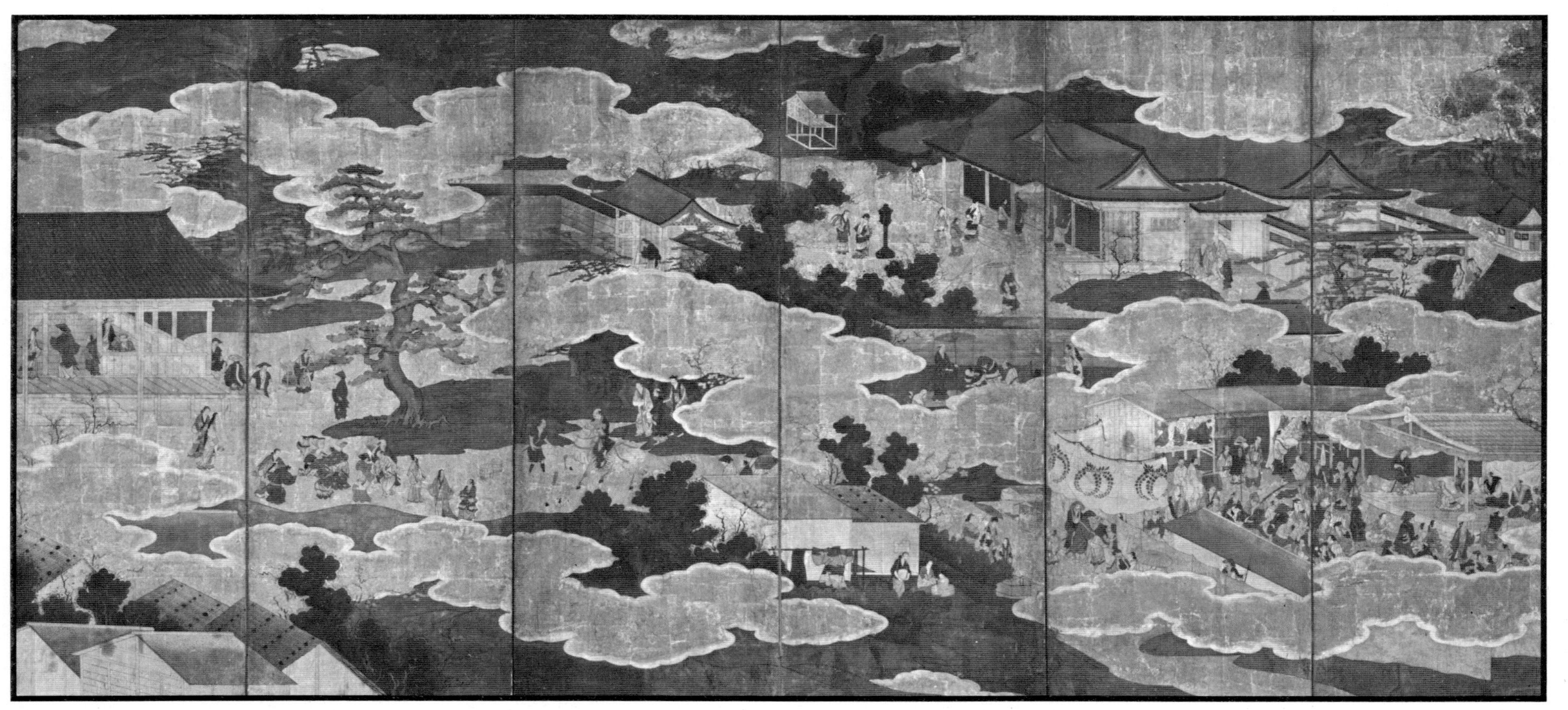

This screen pair, which is sometimes called "Celebrated Places in Kyoto," features the landmarks and landscape of the ancient capital of Kyoto. The right screen,* which depicts the Higashiyama (Eastern Hills) section of the city, includes the Kiyomizu Temple in the upper right. The temple is easily identified because of the distinctive stage-like porch of the main hall that juts out over the mountain on which it was built. The Kiyomizu scene also includes the small Otowa waterfall in the first panel, which is familiar to visitors to the temple today. By a skillful transposition of space made through the use of meandering gold clouds, the scene shifts in the lower half of the screen to the Yasaka Shrine of Gion, which spreads from the center of the painting to the left edge. Around the shrine precincts are men and women who are visiting the shrine. A group of dancers has gathered near the imposing front gate, and the first panel even includes figures dressed as Portuguese.

The left screen, which shows the broad precincts of the Kitano Shrine located in the northern part of Kyoto, is similarly divided into separate scenes by gold clouds. The main shrine building occupies the upper part of the first three panels. Below the shrine proper is a separate stage where an audience has gathered for a performance of Okuni Kabuki (see No. 10). The structure at the extreme left of this screen is the Sutra Repository.

Scenes of Higashiyama and Kitano are thought to be a motif combination common to traditional "famous place pictures" (*meisho-e*), and a number of screen paintings are extant that combine these localities with genre activities and scenes of spring merriments. For example, Chōen-ji, a temple located in Nishio City in Aichi Prefecture, owns a pair of six-fold screens dated to the seventeenth century with essentially the same subject matter. However, the Chōen-ji screens focus attention on the main shrine compounds of Yasaka and Kitano, allowing us a closer view of these sites where people are enjoying red plum blossoms and full-flowering cherry trees. The Chōen-ji screens demonstrate a change in approach to the same subject matter, and they are very important for the careful detailed rendering of the pictorial elements. The screens belonging to the Suntory Museum of Art are believed to date to the Keichō era (1596-1615).[1]

*Screens are read from right to left.

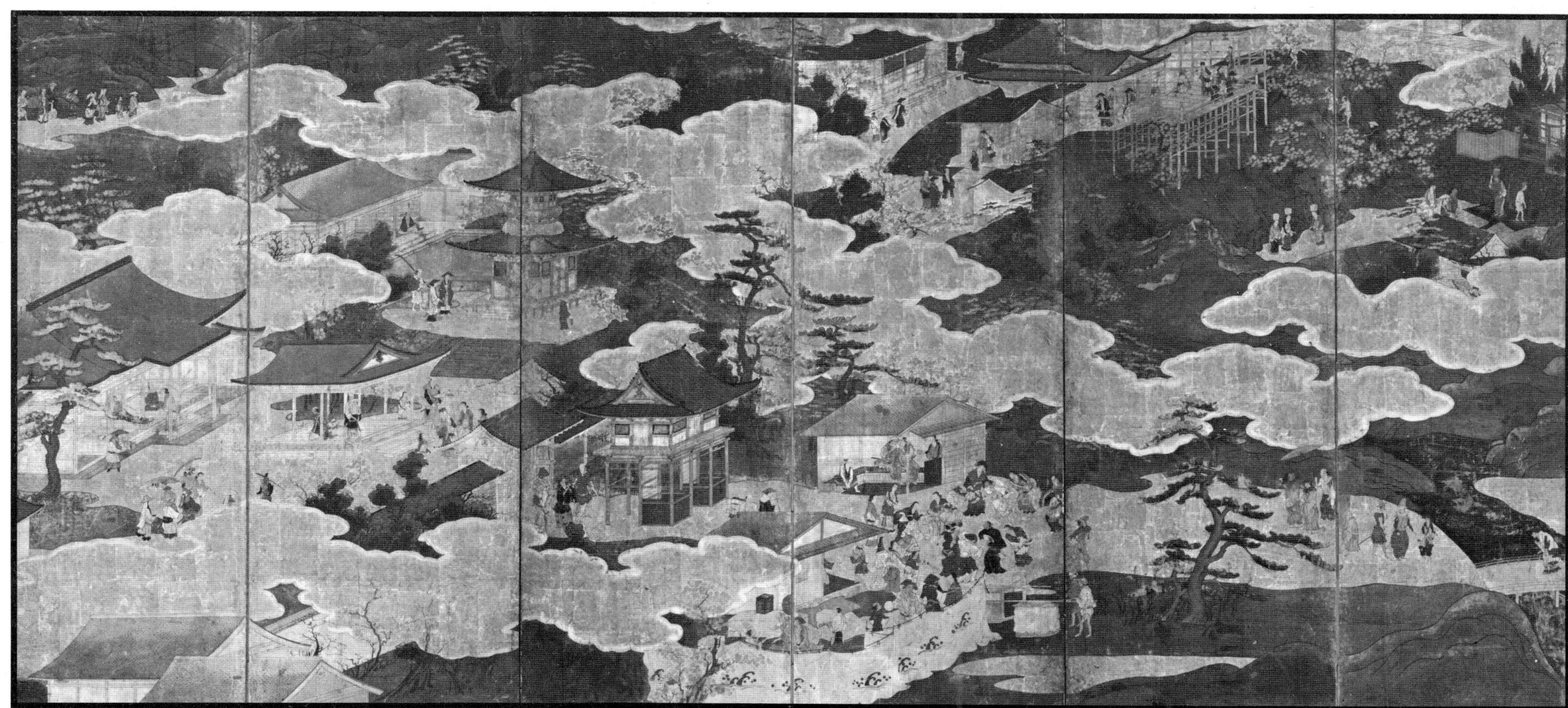

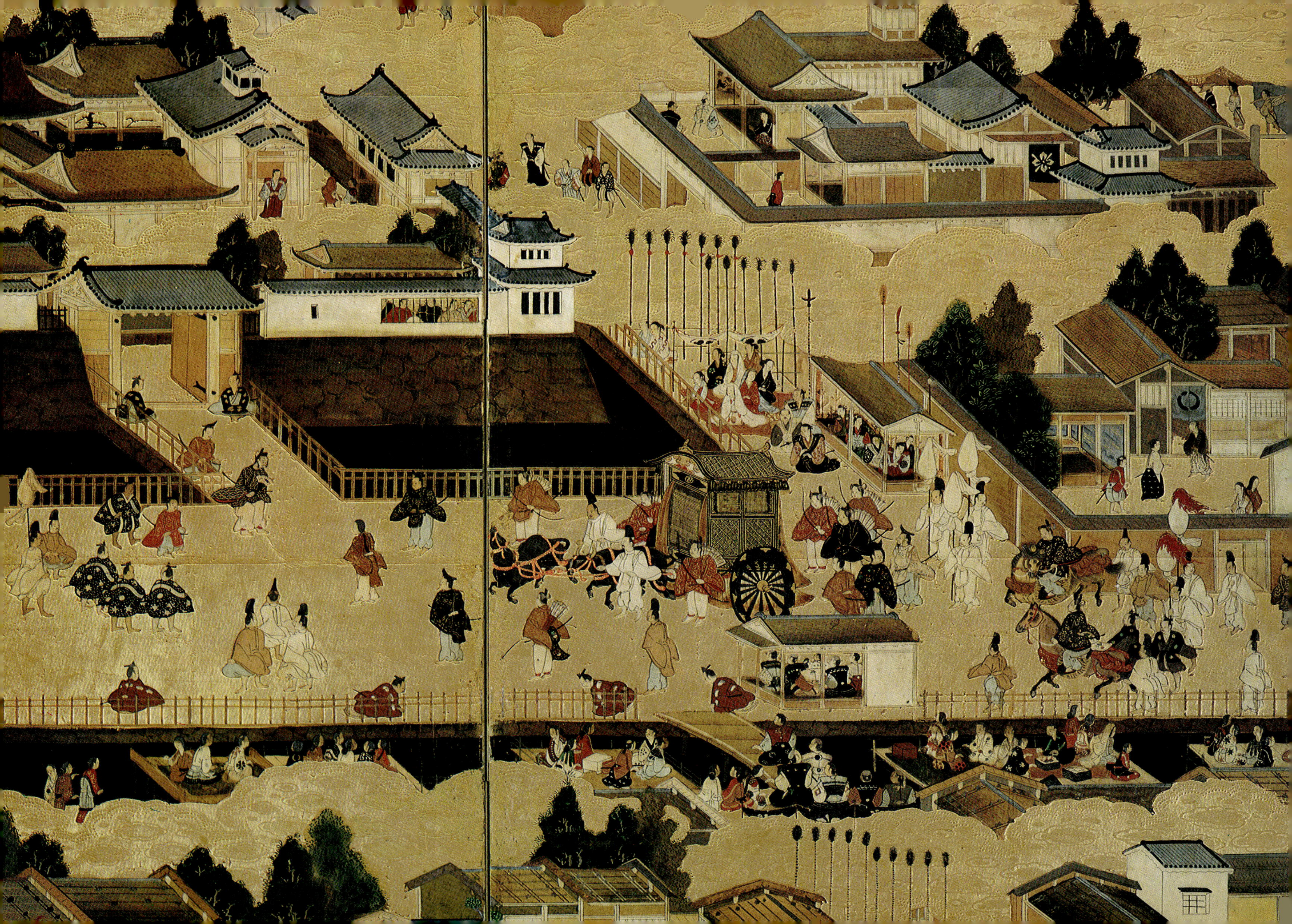

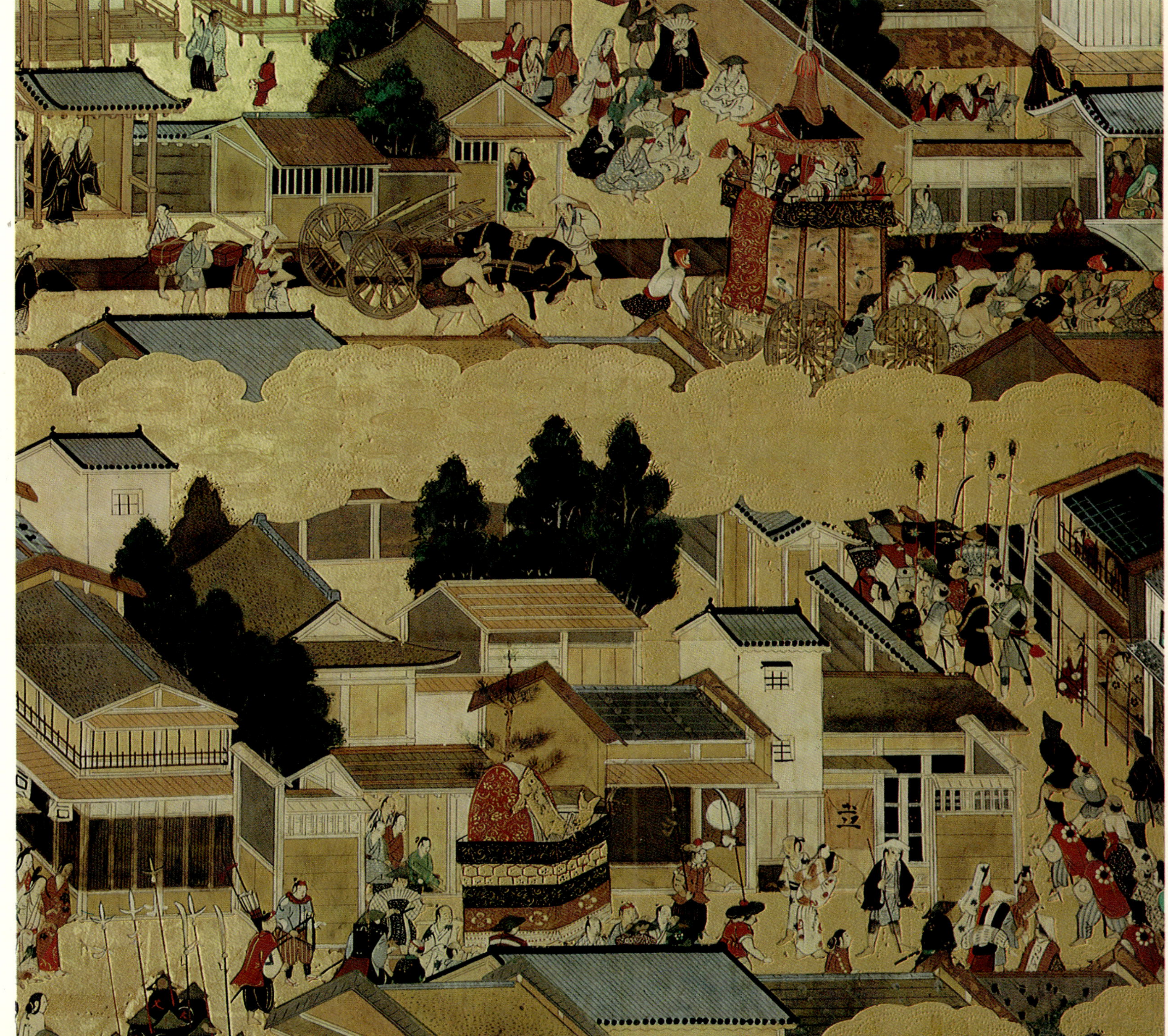

2.
Rakuchū-Rakugai
Detail right screen

2.

RAKUCHŪ-RAKUGAI (Scenes In and Around Kyoto)
Edo period, seventeenth century
Pair of six-fold screens; color and gold on paper
153 cm. x 361.6 cm. each
Signature: "Tosa Fujiwara Mitsutaka," on each screen

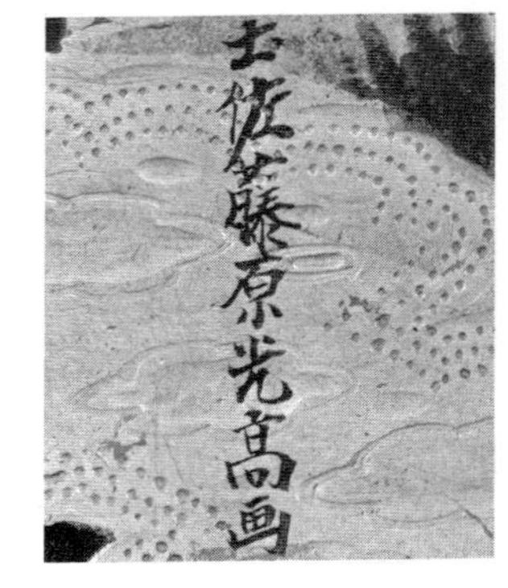

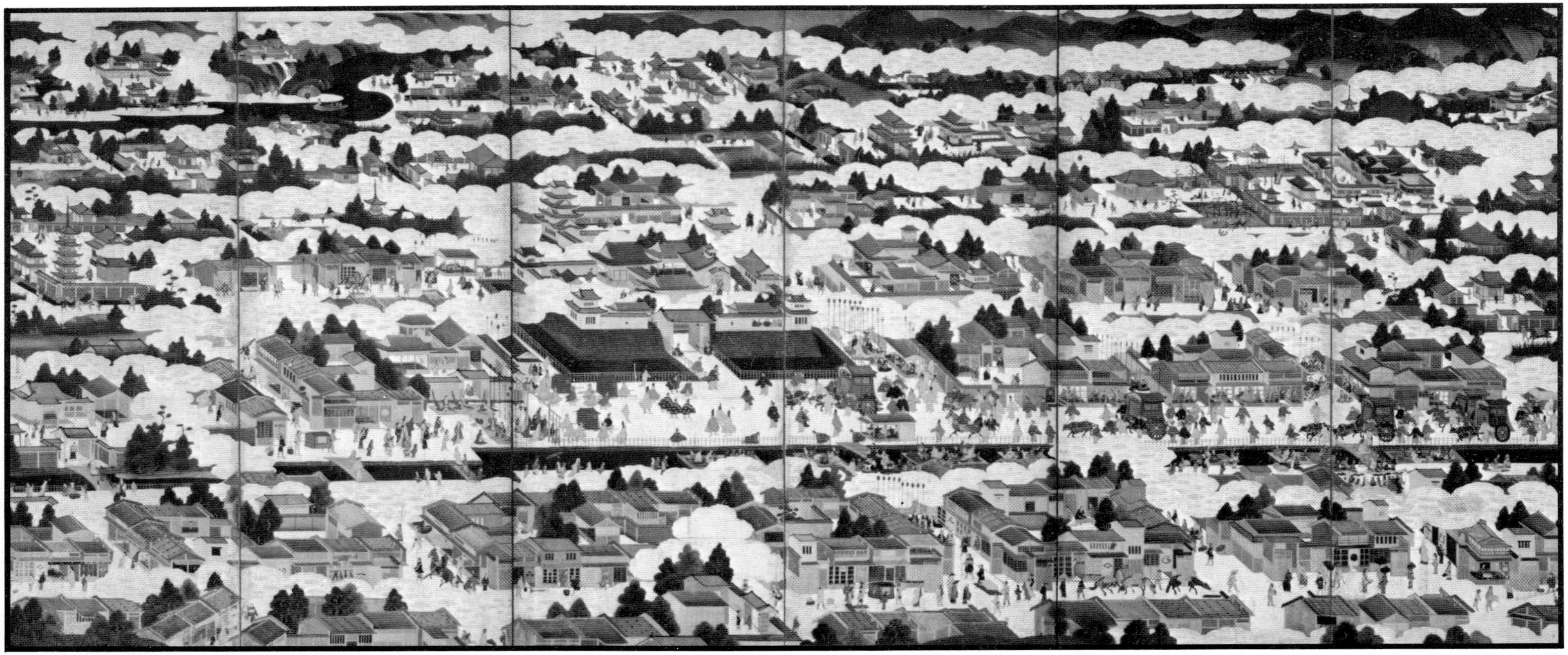

Rakuchū-Rakugai screens are paintings on screen pairs that present large panoramic views of the city of Kyoto and its environs. After their appearance at the beginning of the sixteenth century, this type of screen was produced in large numbers. This "Rakuchū-Rakugai" screen is likely to have been produced to record the visit of the Emperor Gomizuno-o (r. 1611-29) to Nijō Castle in 1626 (6th day, 9th month, 3rd year of Kanei) when a celebration was held to mark the completion of various renovations in the castle structure. This date is an important one in the study of Rakuchū-Rakugai screens because the 1626 renovation removed the multi-storied donjon from the main residence building and placed it to the back of the principal compound. This change in the appearance of Nijō Castle is clearly recorded on Rakuchū-Rakugai paintings, and it is useful, therefore, in dating the screens.

In this screen pair, Nijō Castle is centered on the left screen, while the right screen gives a broad view of the center of the city where the colorful Gion Festival is in progress. The Imperial Palace, deserted after the departure of the imperial carriage, can be seen in the center of the fifth and sixth panels of the right screen. In the left screen, the imperial entourage moves slowly along the Hori River towards Nijō Castle, the large structure in the third and fourth panels. A number of famous temples are scattered across the upper half of each screen. In the right screen the most obvious landmark is the Great Buddha Hall of Hōkō-ji, which was dedicated and built by Toyotomi Hideyoshi in 1591. Above Hōkō-ji is the Hōkoku Shrine, to the right is Sanjūsangen-dō, and just below Hōkō-ji is the bridge that crosses the Kamo River at Gojō Street. The Yasaka Shrine in Gion is centered on the third and

fourth panels of the right screen, with the bustling Shijō-Kawaramachi area below and the bridge at Sanjō Street above. In the left screen the Kitano Shrine is in the upperpart of the first and second panels. The temple at the top of the third panel is Myōshin-ji, and Tō-ji, the great center of esoteric Buddhism, is at the extreme left.

This "Rakuchū-Rakugai" pair has a very orderly composition. The rows of gold clouds are horizontally arranged, and the beauty of this screen pair lies in the clear, explicit presentation of streets, buildings, and figures.[2]

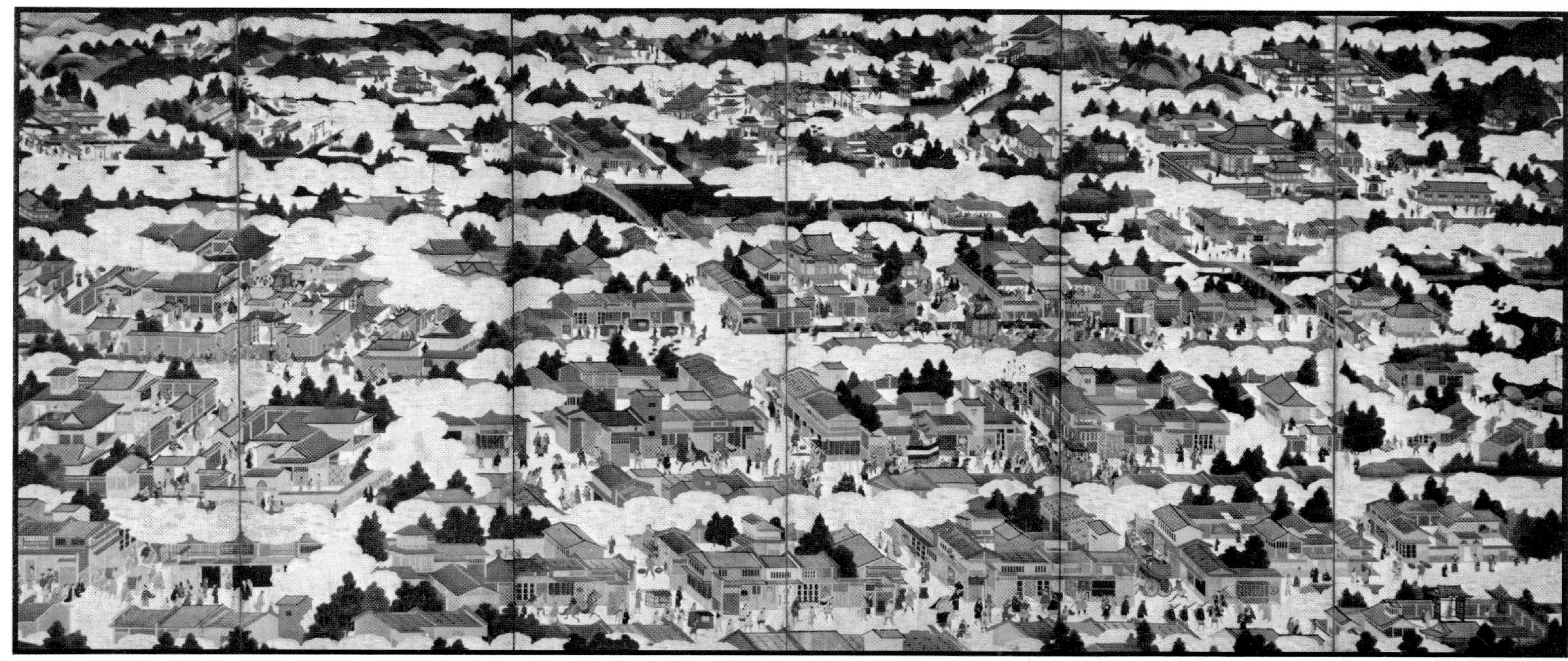

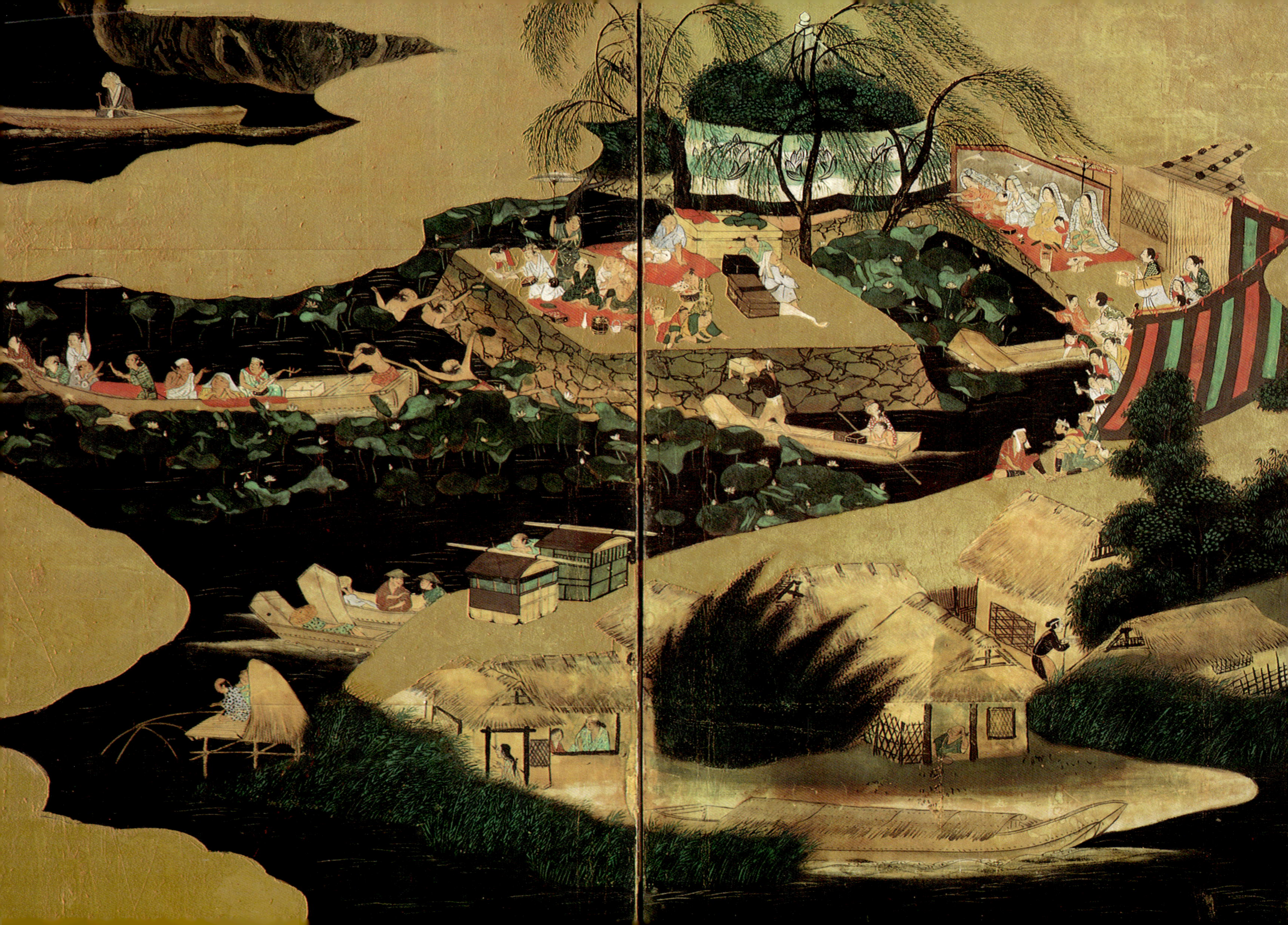

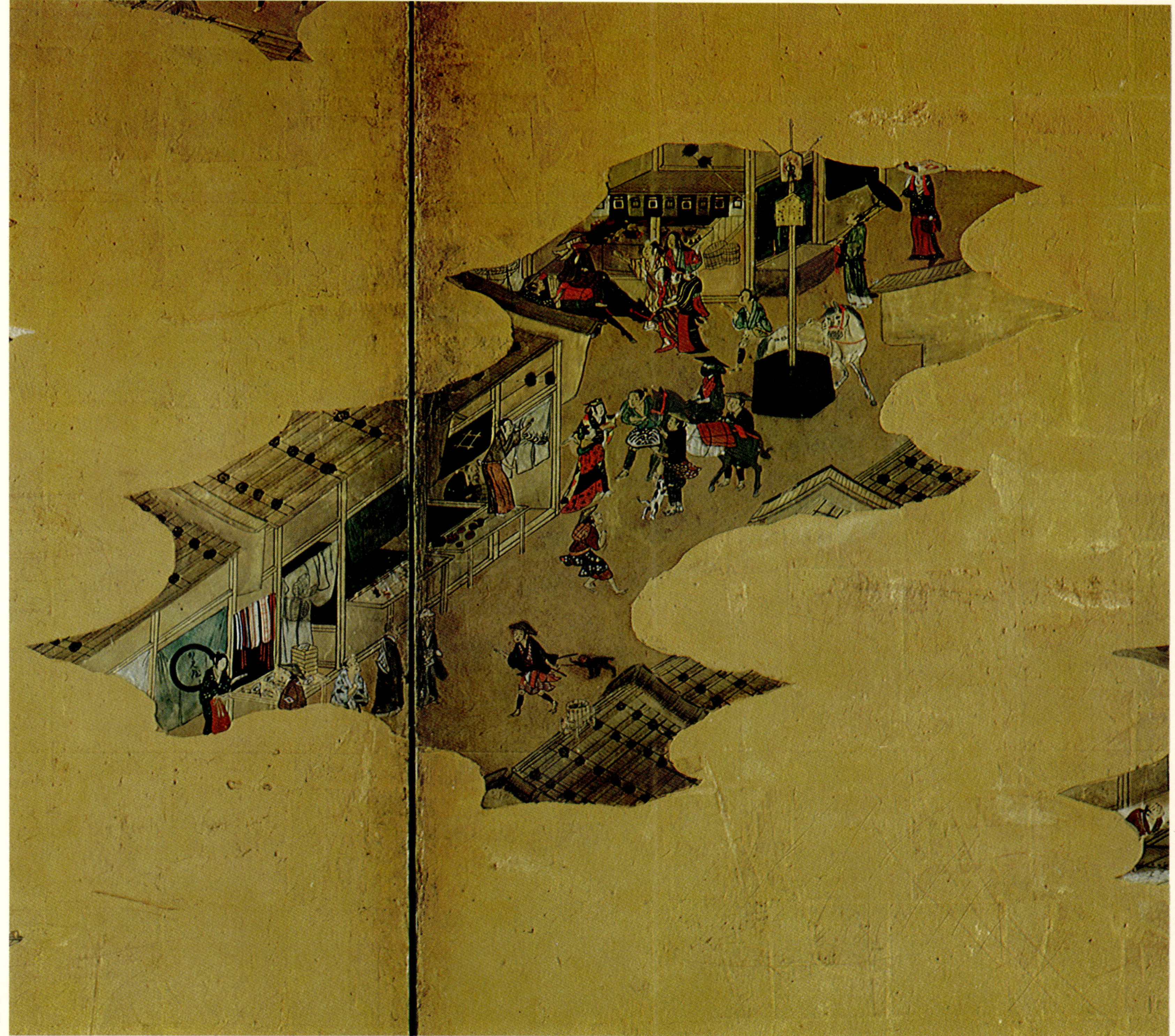

**3. Celebrated Places
in Ōmi Province**
Detail right screen

3.

CELEBRATED PLACES IN ŌMI PROVINCE

Edo period, seventeenth century
Pair of six-fold screens; color and gold on paper
153.2 cm. x 348.4 cm., each

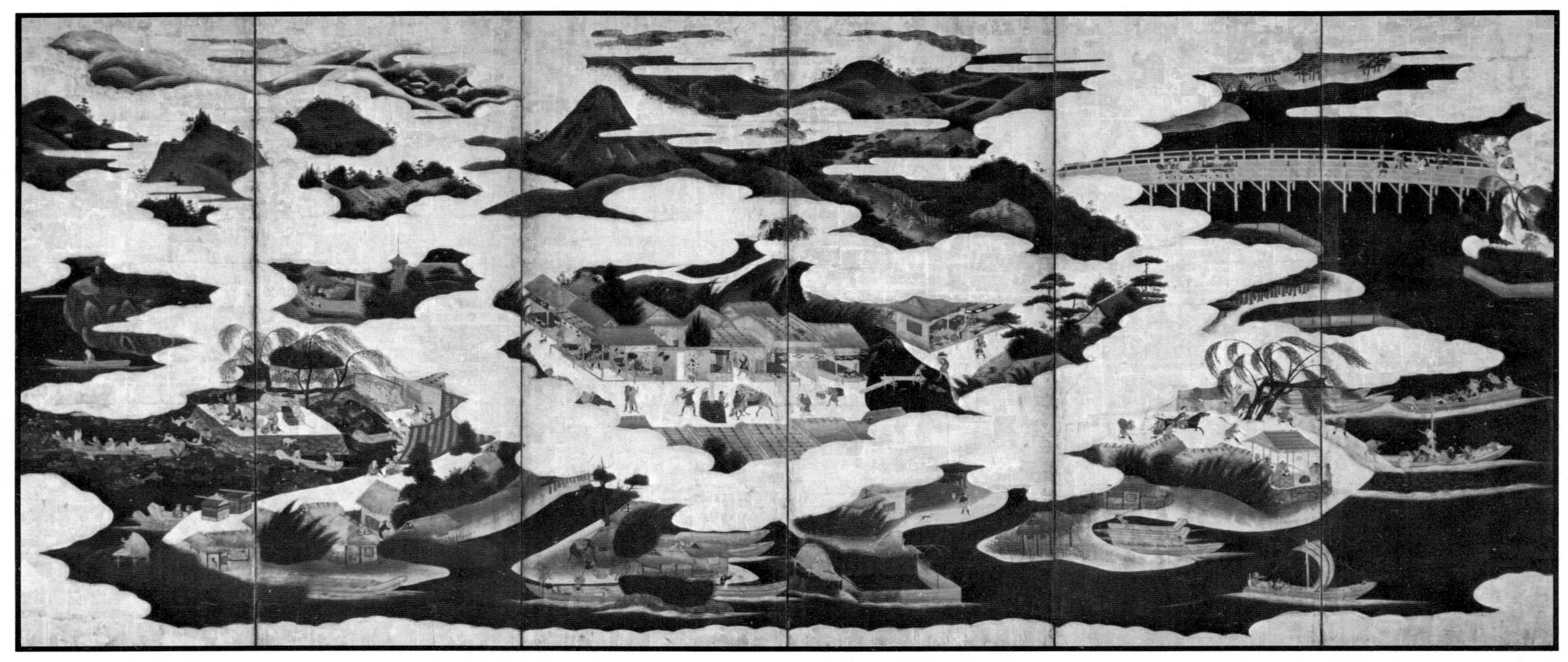

Ōmi is the old provincial name for the area, now Shiga Prefecture, which lies to the east of Kyoto. This unusual screen pair, which depicts a variety of genre activity, features sites surrounding Lake Biwa, Japan's largest lake. Because of its proximity to Kyoto, the Lake Biwa area was developed early in Japan's history, and a number of famous temples are located nearby. During the Momoyama period the area assumed considerable military and economic significance. For example, Oda Nobunaga built Azuchi Castle at the southern tip of Lake Biwa in 1576. Zeze Castle, which was built near Ōtsu City at the beginning of the seventeenth century by Honda Yasutoshi, was the residence of the Honda family throughout the Edo period. Hikone Castle, which still stands, is the name for a castle that was given in 1616 to Ii Naokatsu, a vassal of Tokugawa Ieyasu.

A number of landmarks are included in this screen pair. On the right screen, the Hiyoshi Shrine is at the top of the second panel. Mt. Hiei is visible at the top of the third panel, and the "Pine of Karasaki," a large pine tree that is frequently mentioned in classical poetry, is prominent in the center of the panel. The scenes of Ōtsu City in the fourth and fifth panels include figures of people hawking folk-paintings now commonly known as Ōtsu-e, and the large structure in the extreme left is Zeze Castle, its visible remains now located within Ōtsu City.

The first two panels of the left screen feature a large bridge located in an area called Seta at the southern tip of the lake. The city of Kusatsu spreads over the center two panels of the screen. The prominent mountain above Kusatsu City is Mt. Mikasa, and the distant snow covered mountains in the upper left panels are the peaks of the Hira mountain range.

Scenes of Ōmi Province were frequently arranged and identified on screen paintings in a manner following the theme of the "Shō-shō Hakkei" (Eight Views at the Confluence of the Hsiao and Hsiang Rivers), a very popular theme in traditional Chinese poetry and landscape painting. The "Shō-shō Hakkei" theme provides temporal and climatic associations to established geographical motifs. For example, the pine tree on the right screen is called "Evening Rain Over Karasaki." The bridge on the left screen is identified as "Evening Glow Over Seta Bridge," and the snow covered mountains in the upper left corner of the screen are associated with "Evening Snow Over Mt. Hira."[3]

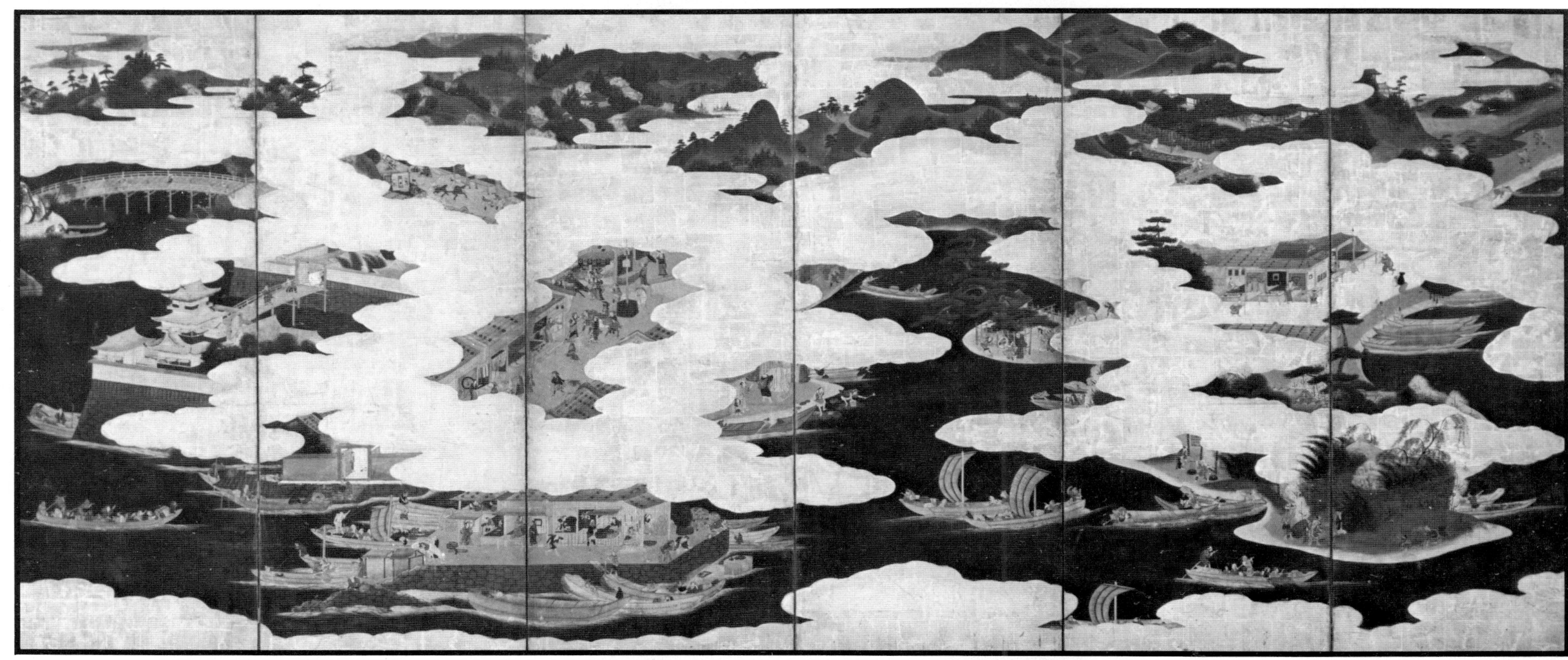

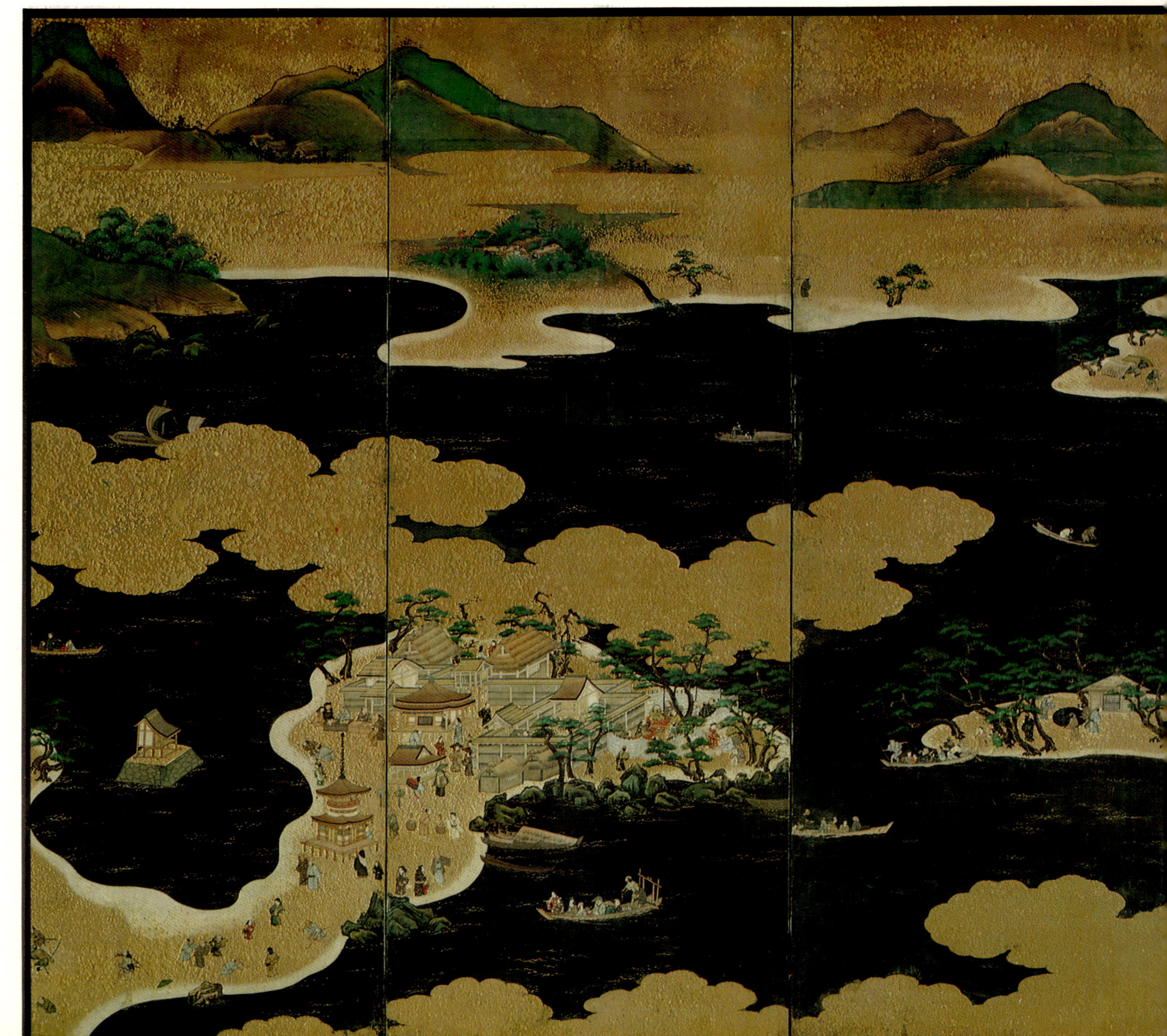

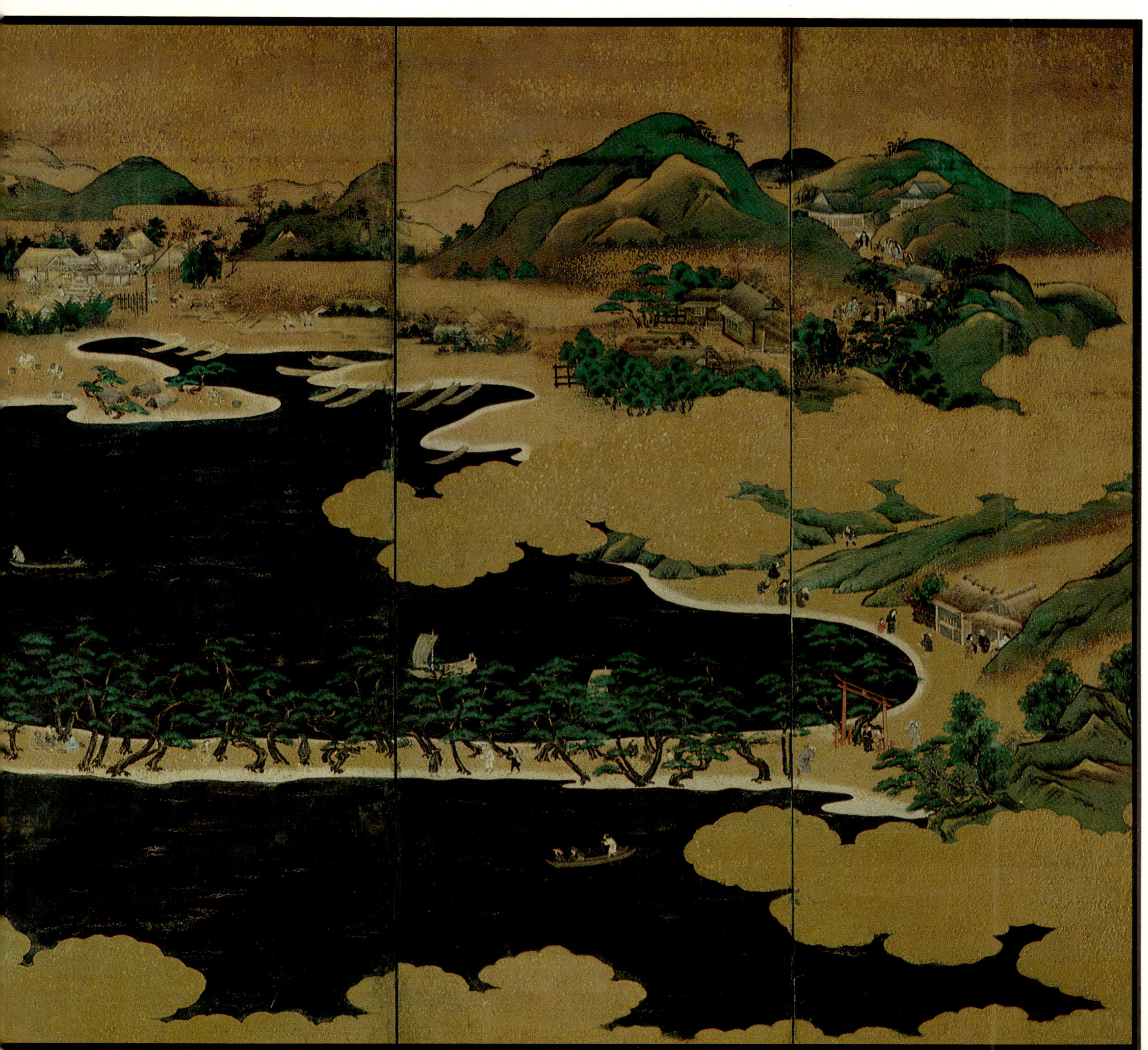

4.
Itsukushima and Ama no Hashidate
Right screen

4.
ITSUKUSHIMA AND AMA NO HASHIDATE
Edo period, seventeenth century
Pair of six-fold screens; color and gold on paper
155.5 cm. x 336 cm. each

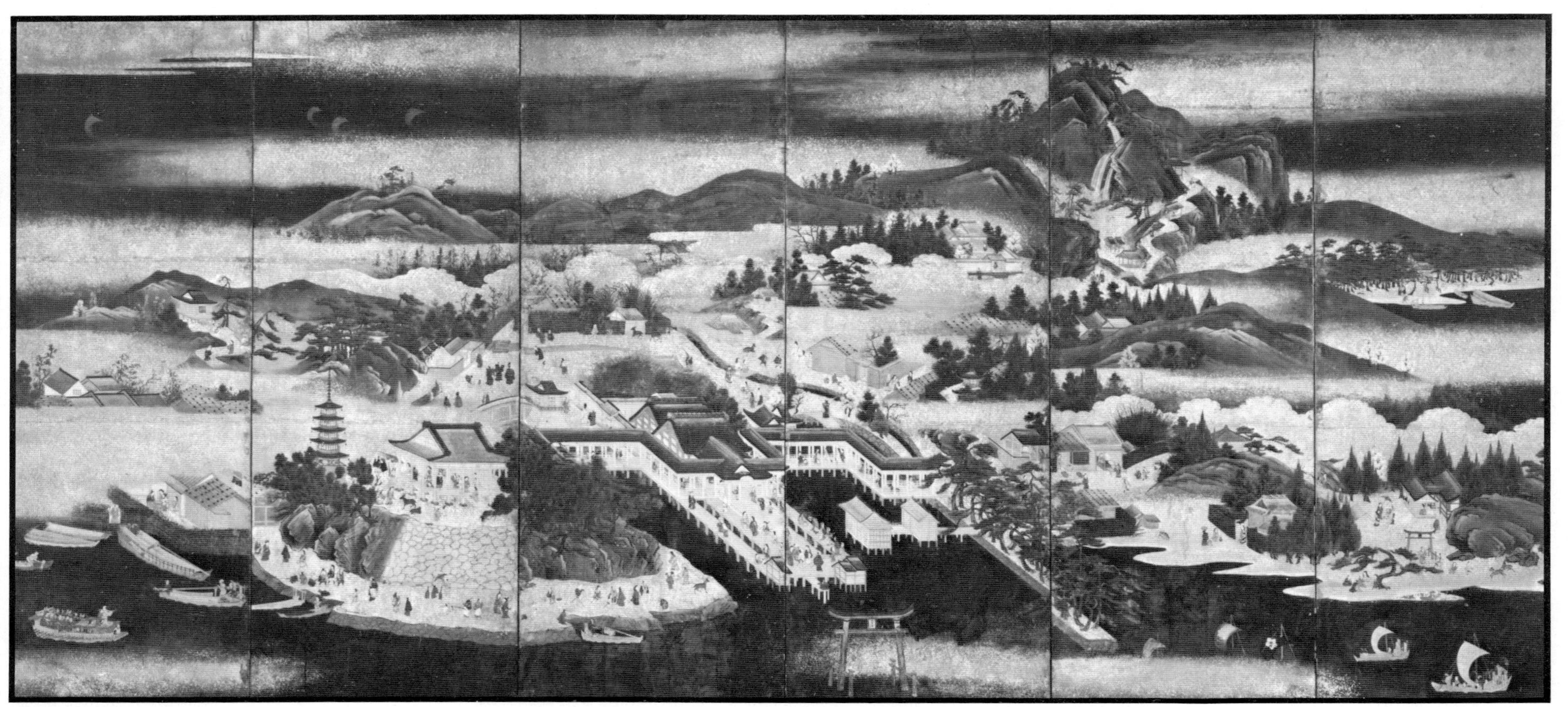

Japan's three most famous scenic spots are Itsu-kushima in Hiroshima Prefecture, Ama no Hashi-date located on the Japan Sea in Kyoto Prefecture, and Matsushima in Miyagi Prefecture. Depictions of these sites were common to the "famous place pictures" *(meisho-e)* of the traditional *Yamato-e* style produced during and after the late Heian period (897-1185). Since screen paintings of famous scenic spots made before the Muromachi period (1334-1568) are not extant, it is not possible to know how those scenes were depicted. However, the tradition of painting these sites survived, and as depictions of the activities of people became more numerous during the Momoyama period, the addi-tion of colorful genre elements to these famous views represents a new development in painting. The Suntory Museum screens which show visitors to Itsukushima and to Ama no Hashidate are representative of this development.

The Itsukushima Shrine, built on the shore of the small island of Miyajima just off the coast of Hiroshima, was the tutelary shrine of the Heian general, Taira no Kiyomori (1118-81) and his family. This painting presents the shrine much as it appears to visitors today. At full tide the shrine and the *torii* gate that stands before it appear to float on the water. The red of the shrine buildings and the green of the island are reflected on the surface of the water in a splendid display of color contrasts.

Ama no Hashidate is a sandbar that stretches for about two kilometers into a bay facing the Japan Sea. This memorable scene is most familiar to the West through a celebrated ink painting of the site by the Muromachi period painter, Sesshū (1420-1506). In this screen the sandbar is skillfully depicted with visitors strolling beneath its stand of twisted pines. To the left of the sandbar is a carefully drawn temple known as the Monju-dō which is located on a promontory opposite the sandbar.

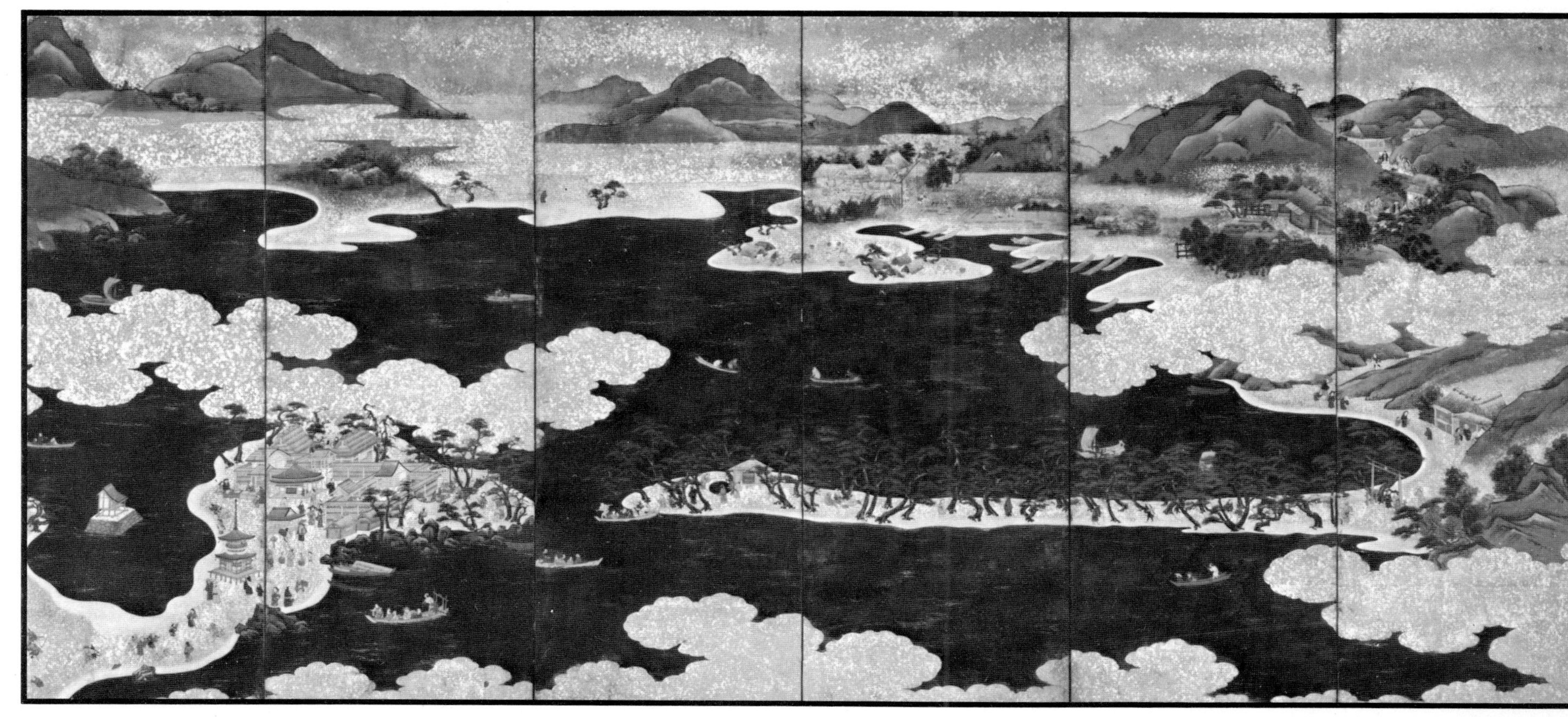

5.
SUMIDA RIVER
Edo period
by Kuwagata Keisai (1764-1824)
Eight-fold screen; ink and light color on paper
152 cm. x 438 cm.
Signature: "Keisai" (with date of " aday in the 5th month, 8th cyclical year,
sign of the serpent, 4th year of Bunsei era"; 1821)
Seal: "Shōshin"

Keisai, who was also called Kitao Masayoshi, was a student of the *ukiyo-e* painter, Kitao Shigemasa (1739–1820). Keisai began as an *ukiyo-e* illustrator. By 1780 he was producing drawings for *kibyoshi,* small picture books with yellow paper covers consisting primarily of pictures but in which a story is carried with conversation and simple explanations. The number of Keisai's works of this type extant exceed one hundred sixty pieces. Keisai later studied with the Kanō school and was influenced by the decorative works of the Rimpa artist, Ogata Kōrin (1658–1716). He also mastered a number of other painting styles including techniques of Western painting.

When Keisai stopped designing *ukiyo-e* in 1797, he changed his name to Kuwagata Keisai and concentrated on his own painting style which is characterized by an accomplished and agile brush technique. A handscroll called *Kinsei Shokunin Zukushi E-kotoba* (Scroll III), which belongs to the Tokyo National Museum, is a work of 1805 containing examples of Keisai's individual style.

Keisai was a noted painter of scenes of Edo, and this screen is a work of his very late years. The view presented here focuses on a portion of the Sumida River facing west. The long foreground area is a section of the river bank in the Mukōjima section of the city which was famous for its cherry trees. In this painting the season is spring, and local people are out viewing the fully blossomed trees. On the opposite bank of the river the right section of the screen is the area known as Hashiba, the center section is Imado, and to the left is Asakusa. Sensō-ji, a temple still active today in the Asakusa section, is visible in the seventh panel, and the large faintly drawn mountain in the center distance is Mt. Fuji. Directly below Mt. Fuji along the banks of the river are long racks dotted with black which represent the drying of *"Asakusa-nori,"* a seaweed which was a favorite food of the Edo citizenry.[4]

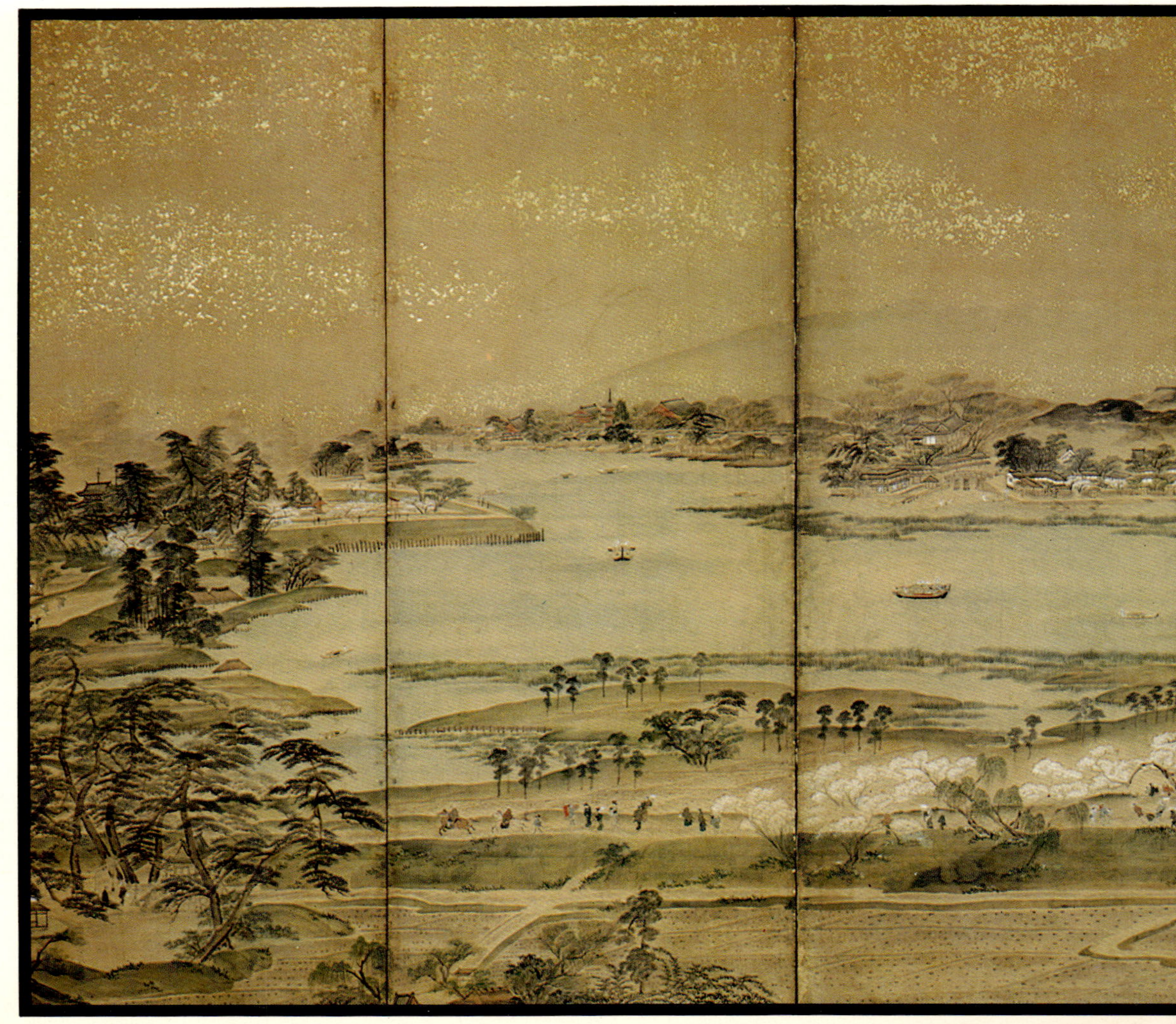

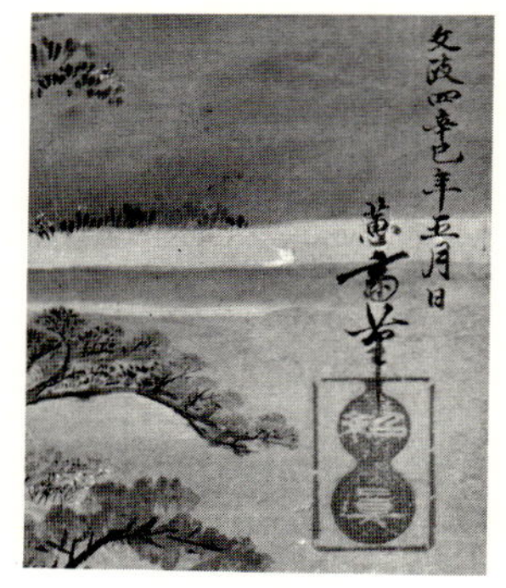

文政四年辛巳年五月日
薫斎筆

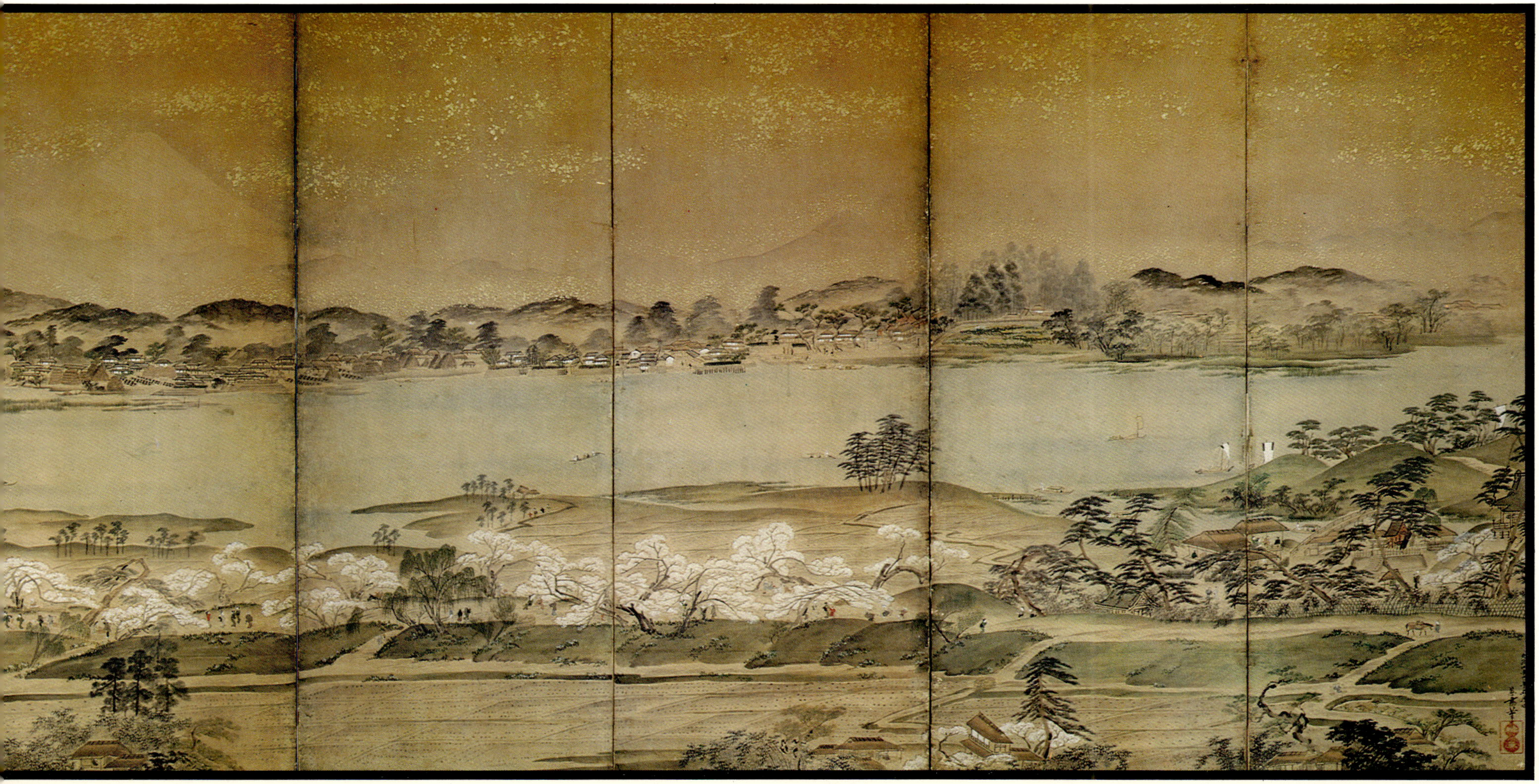

6.
MERRYMAKING UNDER THE CHERRY BLOSSOMS
Momoyama period, seventeenth century
Pair of six-fold screens; color and gold on paper
151 cm. x 352 cm., each
Seals: "Amagi Sōchū," on each screen

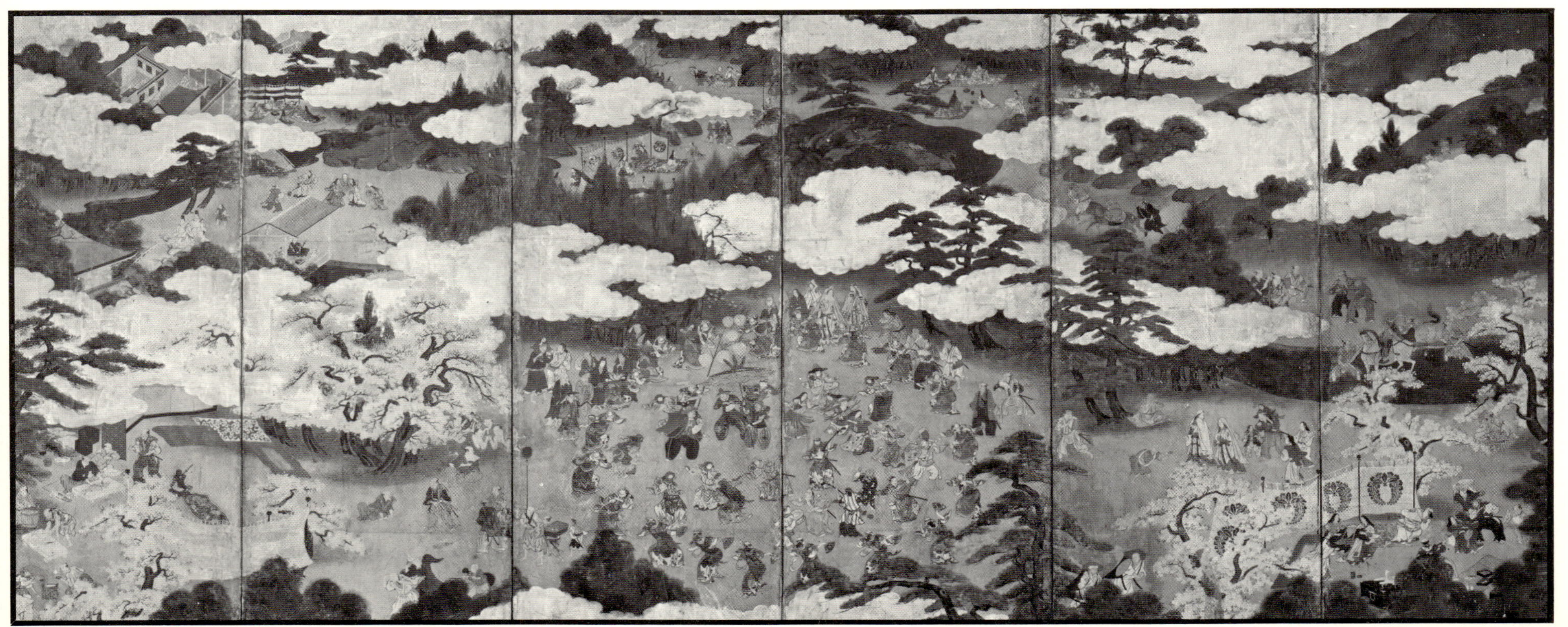

This screen pair shows scenes of Kyoto in spring as people of all classes of society enjoy themselves under cherry trees in full bloom at the Yasaka and Kamigamo shrines. In both screens attention is centered upon a circle of dancers engaged in the *fūryū-odori,* a popular dance in the late sixteenth and early seventeenth centuries. The term, *"fūryū,"* which has a basic meaning of "stylish" or "elegant," later took on the meaning of a "showy device" or "unusual plan." When the term was applied to a dance it meant a dance both fashionable and colorful, and one performed with a conscious attempt to present something new.

In Kyoto various *fūryū-odori* dance groups were formed within neighborhoods, costumes were designed, and contests held. In the right screen, for example, which has the Kamigamo Shrine in the background, the circle of dancers has at its center figures that appear from their dress to be *Nambanjin* or Portuguese (see No. 17), one of whom is carrying a long handled umbrella known as a *fūryū* umbrella. However, these are probably local people in costume and not actual foreigners.

Although the dance is the major motif of each screen, both screens include smaller groups of figures who are viewing the blossoms privately. A group of people in the sixth panel of the right screen appear to be preparing for the visit of an important military general. Notable in this group is the figure of a cook with a kitchen knife in hand. In the left screen, which has the Yasaka Shrine in Gion in the background, the ladies at the right play a game of *sugoroku* or Japanese backgammon, and the other people, dressed as members of the nobility, sip *sake* while watching the gaiety of the dancers.[5]

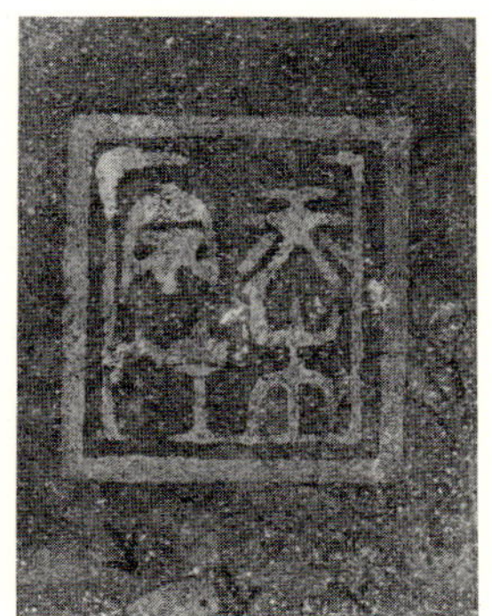

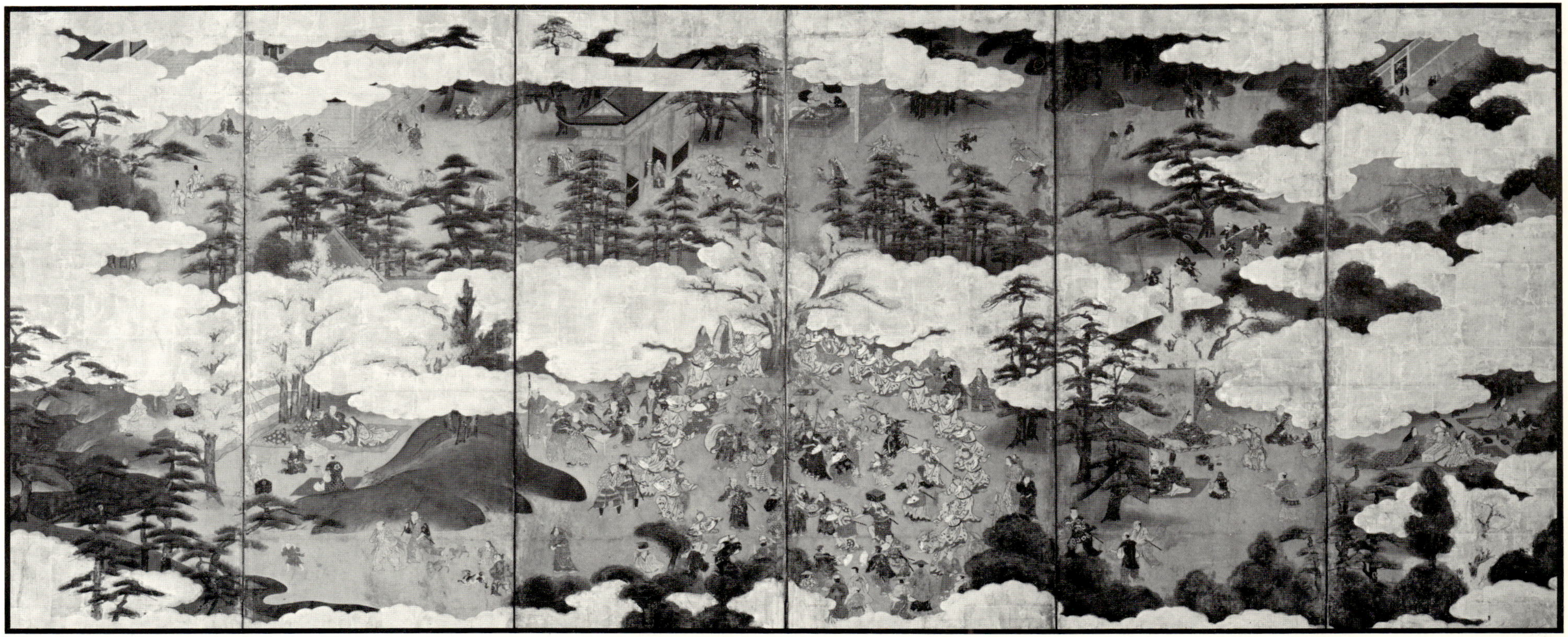

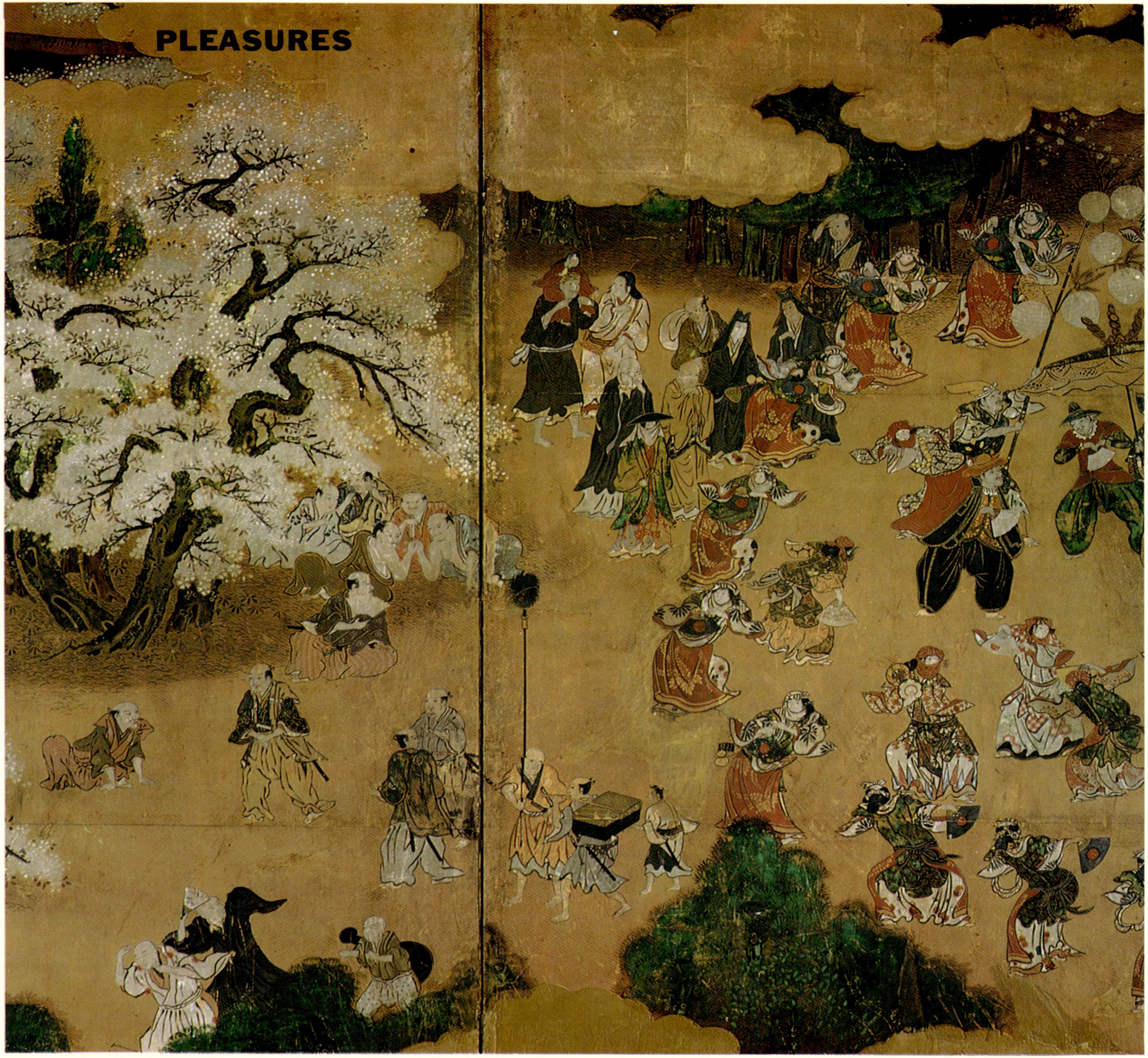

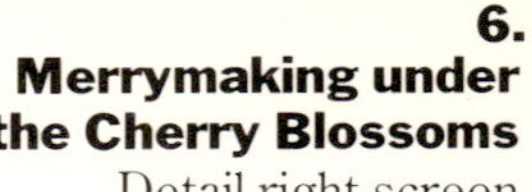

6.
**Merrymaking under
the Cherry Blossoms**
Detail right screen

6.
**Merrymaking under
the Cherry Blossoms**
Detail left screen

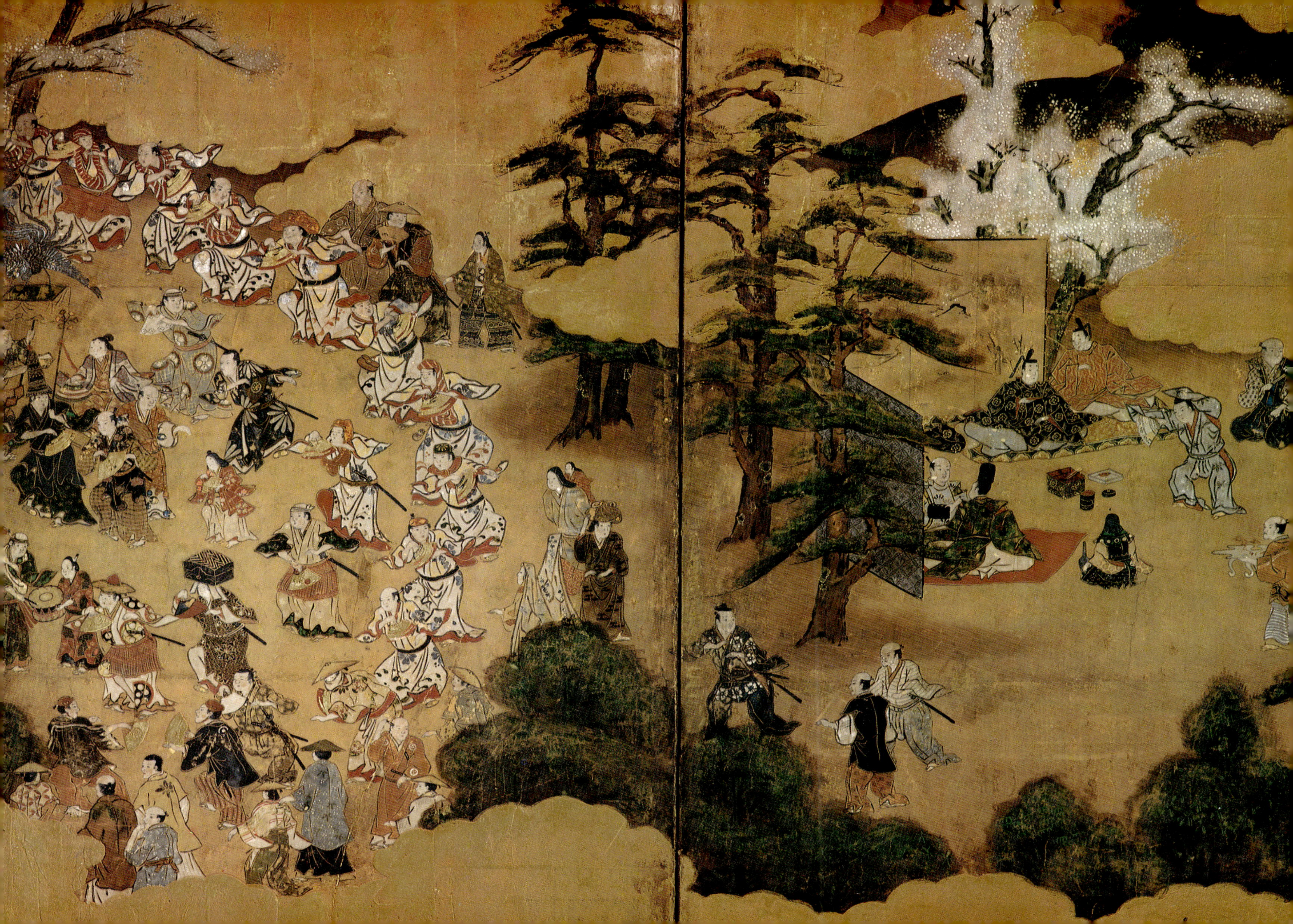

7.
NEW YEAR'S AMUSEMENTS
Edo period, seventeenth century
Six-fold screen; color and gold on paper
122.2 cm. x 258.6 cm.

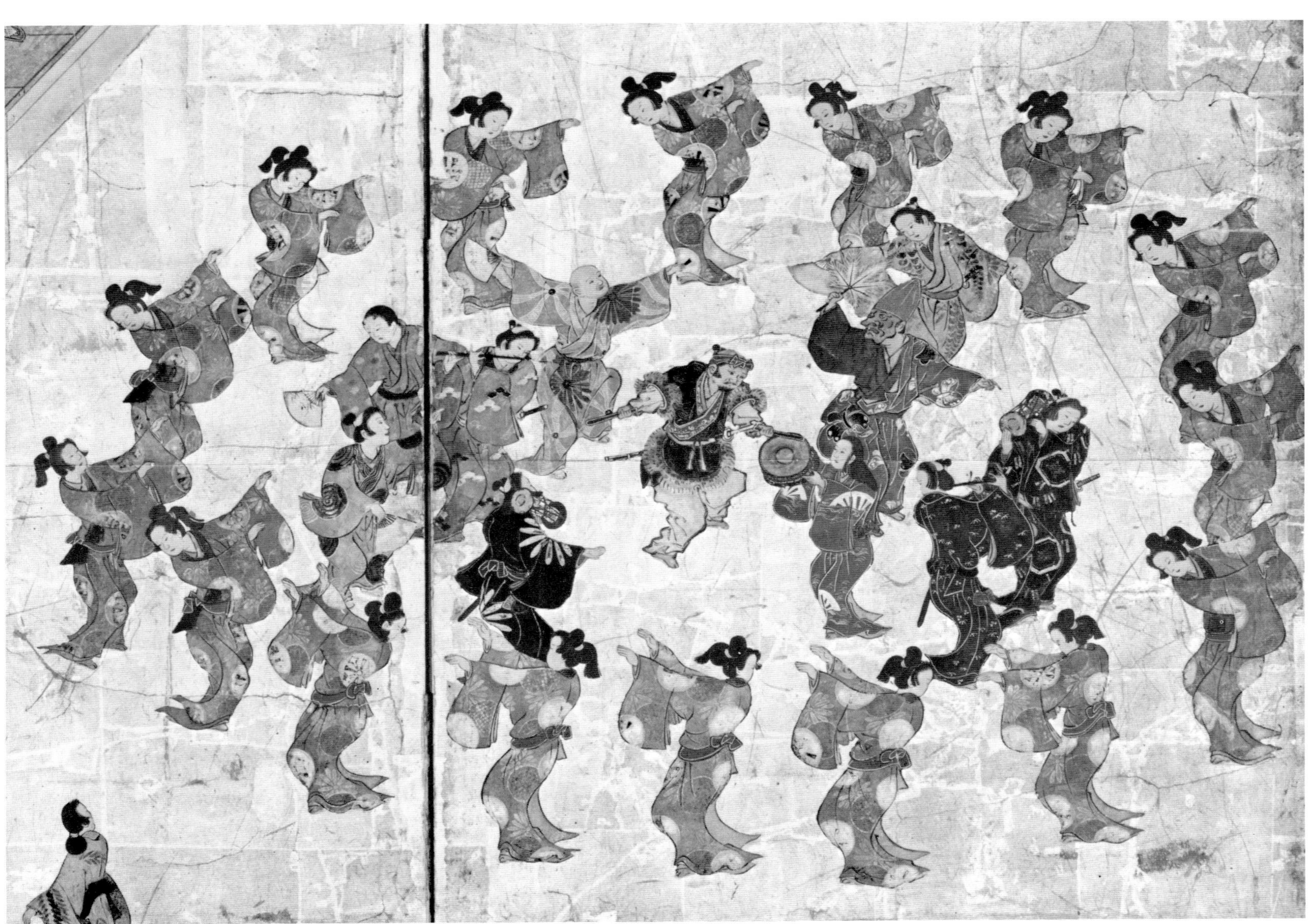

Basic to the traditional *Yamato-e* painting from the Heian period are the forms called *shiki-e* and *tsukinami-e* which take, respectively, as their motifs the landscapes of the four seasons and activities of the twelve months. When these paintings are divided into scenes appropriate to the separate twelve months of the year, the first subject to appear is New Year's festivities. One of the characteristics of the genre painting in the seventeenth century is that in paintings of seasonal activities genre elements take precedence over seasonal motifs.

This small screen painting is an unusual work that shows the various games, sports, and amusements enjoyed during the New Year's holidays. The setting is a large house open to the interior and a courtyard. The focus of activity is a group of young female dancers who wear the *furisode,* or long sleeved kimono. The dancers encircle a group of musicians who play large drums, small drums, and flutes while other dancers keep the rhythm with fans. Further musical accompaniment is provided by musicians seated on the veranda to the left who play the *samisen* (a long-necked, three-stringed instrument), *koto* (a zither-like instrument), and drums. The young people to the right of the dancers play with battledore and shuttlecock. A young boy seated at the corner of the veranda to the left practices archery. In the interior of the house a game of *go* is in progress, and on the veranda directly above the circle of dancers a group of girls play *kai-awase,* or "matching shells." *Kai-awase* was a traditional New Year's game popular from the Heian period. The interiors of three hundred sixty pairs of clam shells are painted with designs, one design per pair. Each design may be an allusion to a classic literary work such as the *Tale of Genji.* The shells are shuffled, divided, and turned over one by one. The object of the game is to match the designs, and when all shells have been matched, the person with the most pairs wins.

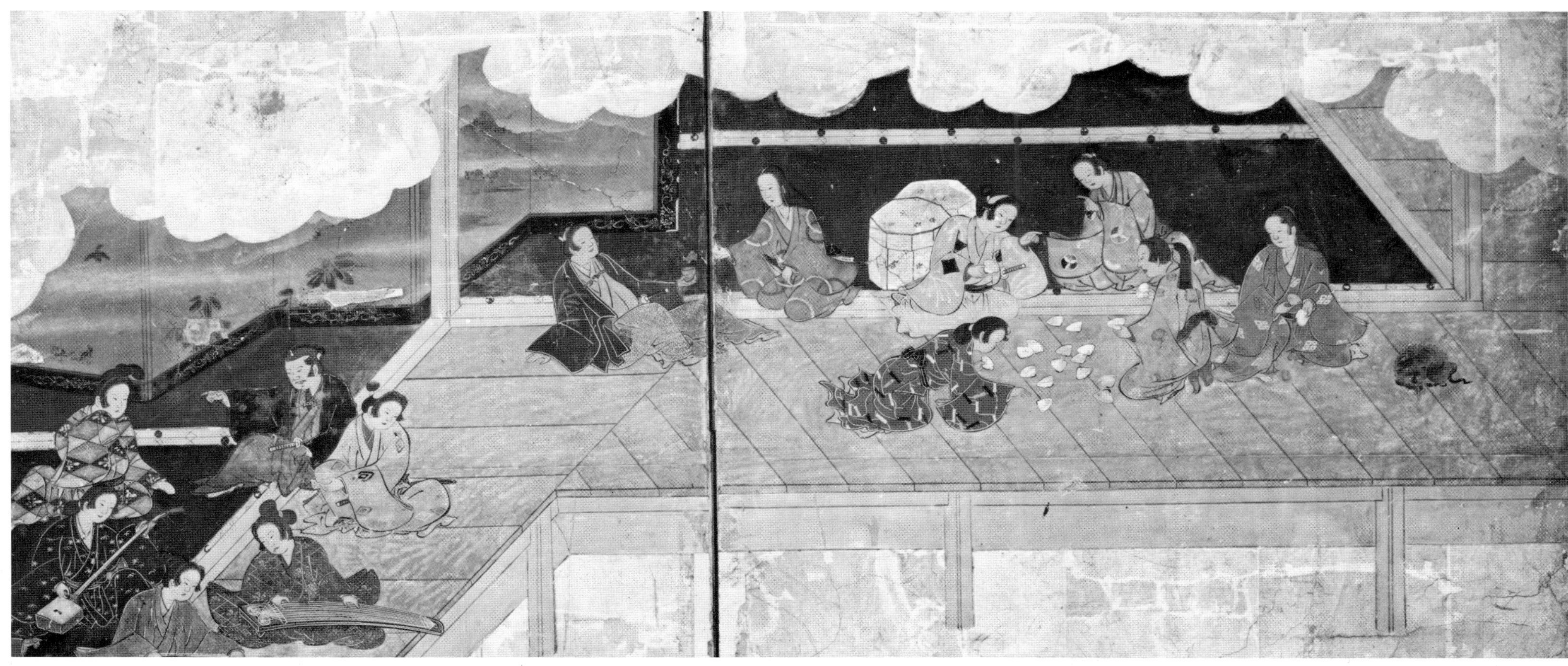

7.
New Year's Amusements

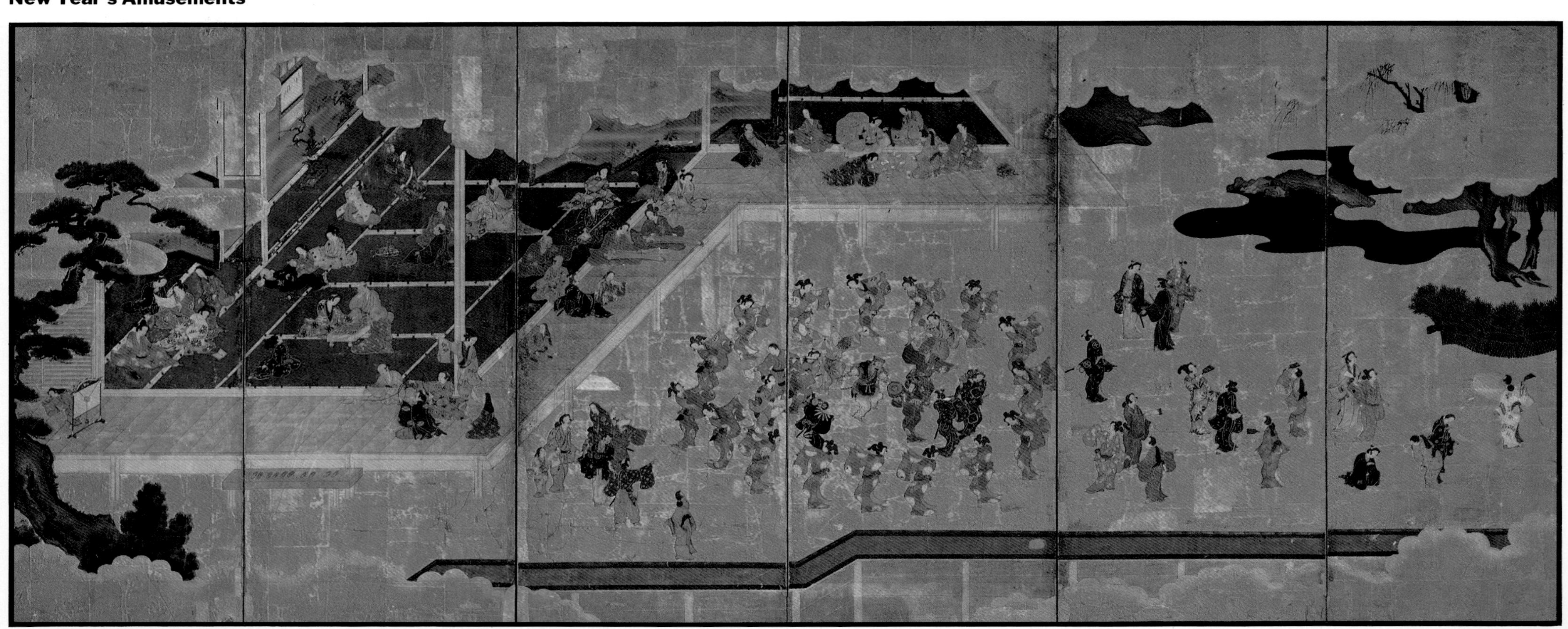

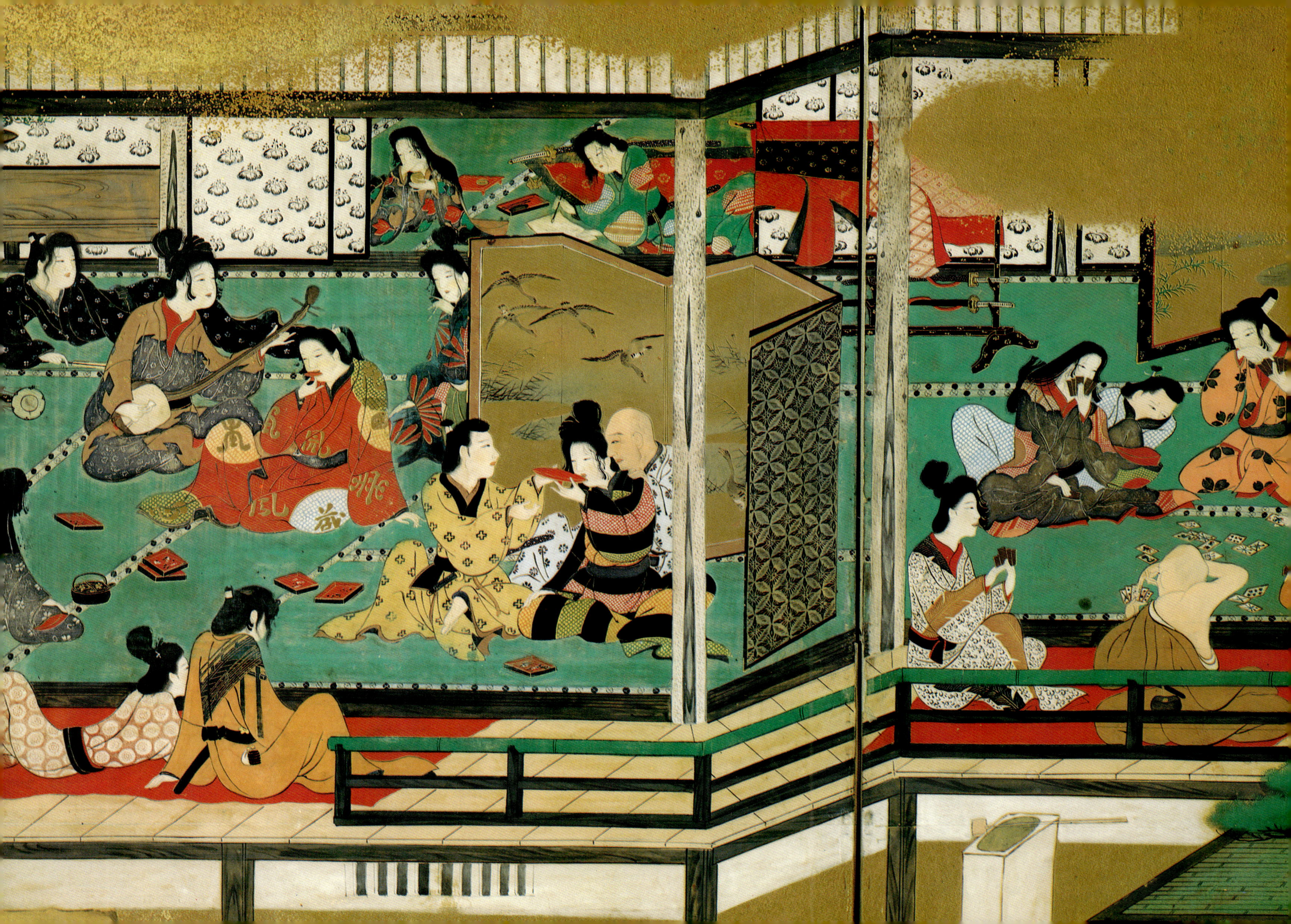

8.
ENTERTAINMENTS AT A HOUSE OF PLEASURE
Edo period, seventeeth century
Six-fold screen; color and gold on paper
94.6 cm. x 285.7 cm.

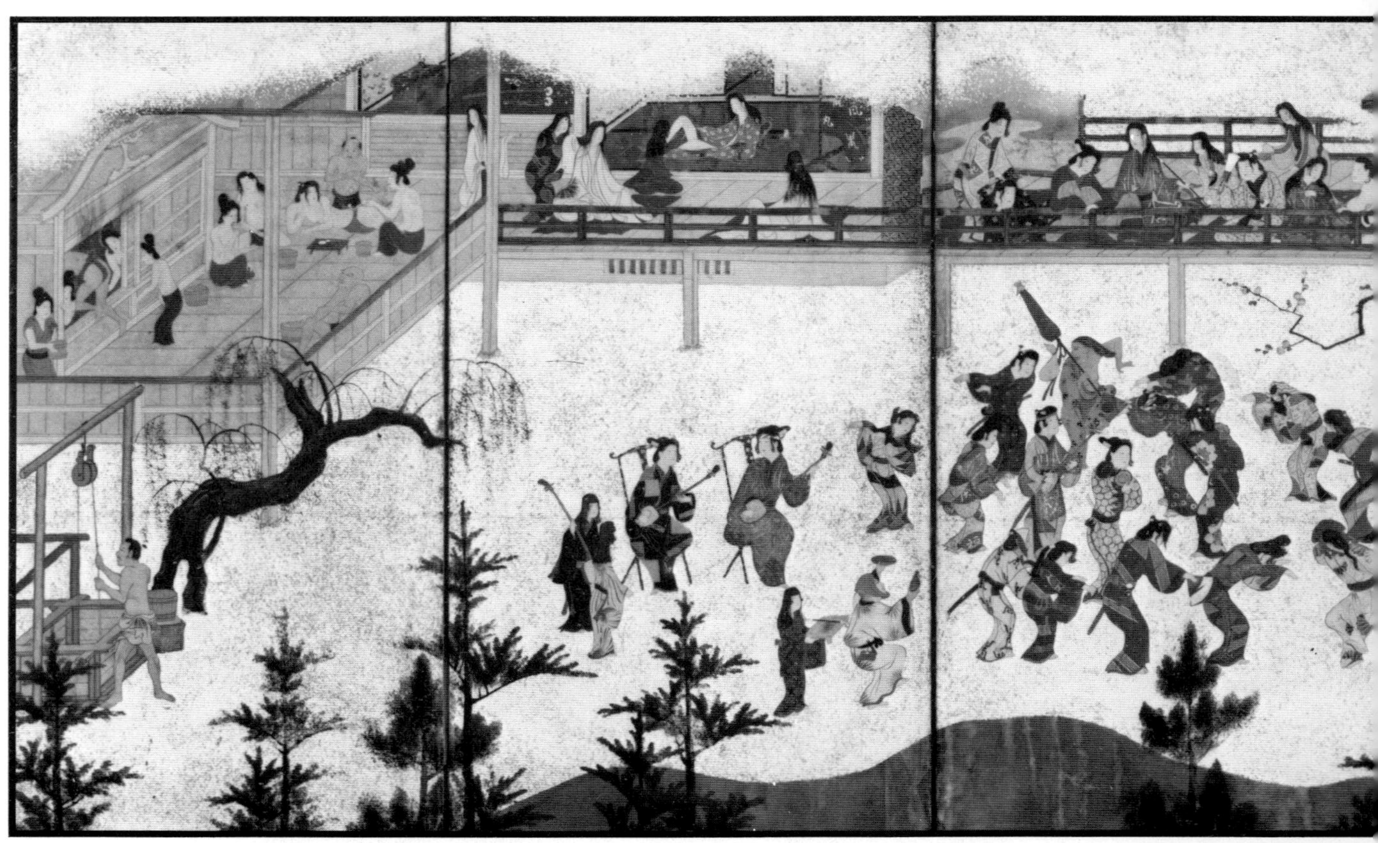

Genre screens produced in the seventeenth century are not limited to scenes set outdoors, but also include screens that show people relaxing or being entertained inside mansions or residences. This was a popular subject of genre painting in which, compared to outdoor scenes, backgrounds are limited. People's activities become the obvious focal point, and the artist is careful to depict these activities and specific amusements faithfully. Moreover, in order to present such scenes adequately, the artist had to create large imaginatively constructed houses as backgrounds. This small but beautiful screen of entertainments is representative of one type of indoor genre painting.

In this screen we see the portion of a large house that faces a courtyard. The main room of the building, which occupies the first three panels, is separated into two compartments by a folding screen painted with geese and reeds, a popular subject with artists who worked in Chinese ink painting styles. At the extreme right of the first panel a *kamuro,* young girl who is employed to serve courtesans, prepares ceremonial tea. Behind her a group of people, including the conspicuous figure of a bare shouldered and shaved priest, play a card game called *un sun karuta,* which is thought to have been inspired by the introduction of Portuguese playing cards *(um sum carta)* in the early seventeenth century. The larger section of this room, in the second and third panels, has a raised alcove *(tokonoma)* at left rear and a window alcove *(shoin)* on the left side. In this room a banquet is in full swing. Guests relax as a courtesan dances to the accompaniment of a musical instrument called a *samisen.* Two men seated in front of the standing screen urge even more *sake* on their companion, and visible behind this screen in a separate room is a man writing a letter.

The early spring season is indicated by the blossoming plum tree and the small new leaves of the willow in the garden. A lively circle of dancers enclose two of the musicians, a woman with a drum and a man playing the *samisen,* while additional accompaniment is provided by two *samisen* players seated in chairs. A bathhouse is attached to this mansion at the left where half nude figures of bathhouse women and their guests sip *sake* and relax in a warm after-bath glow.[6]

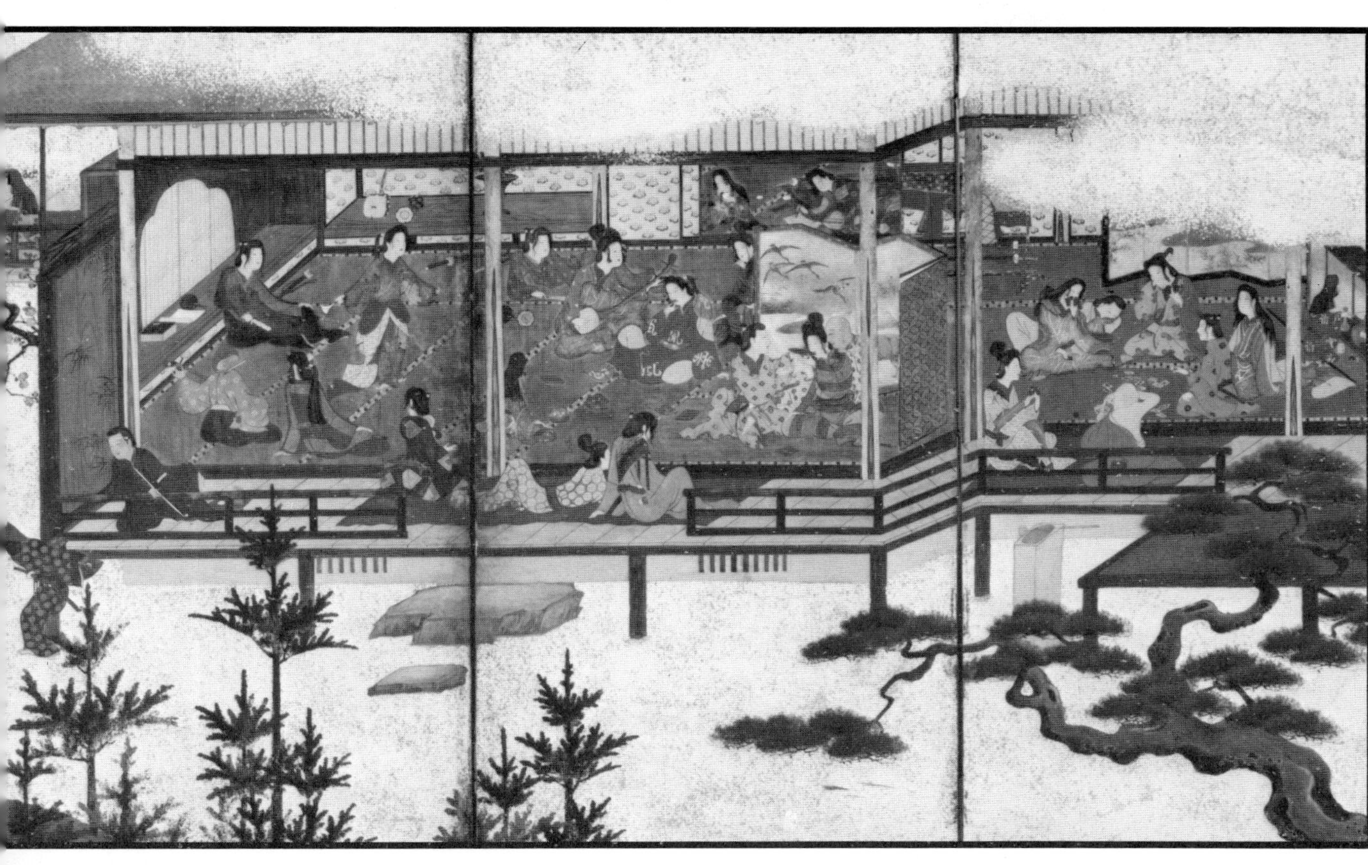

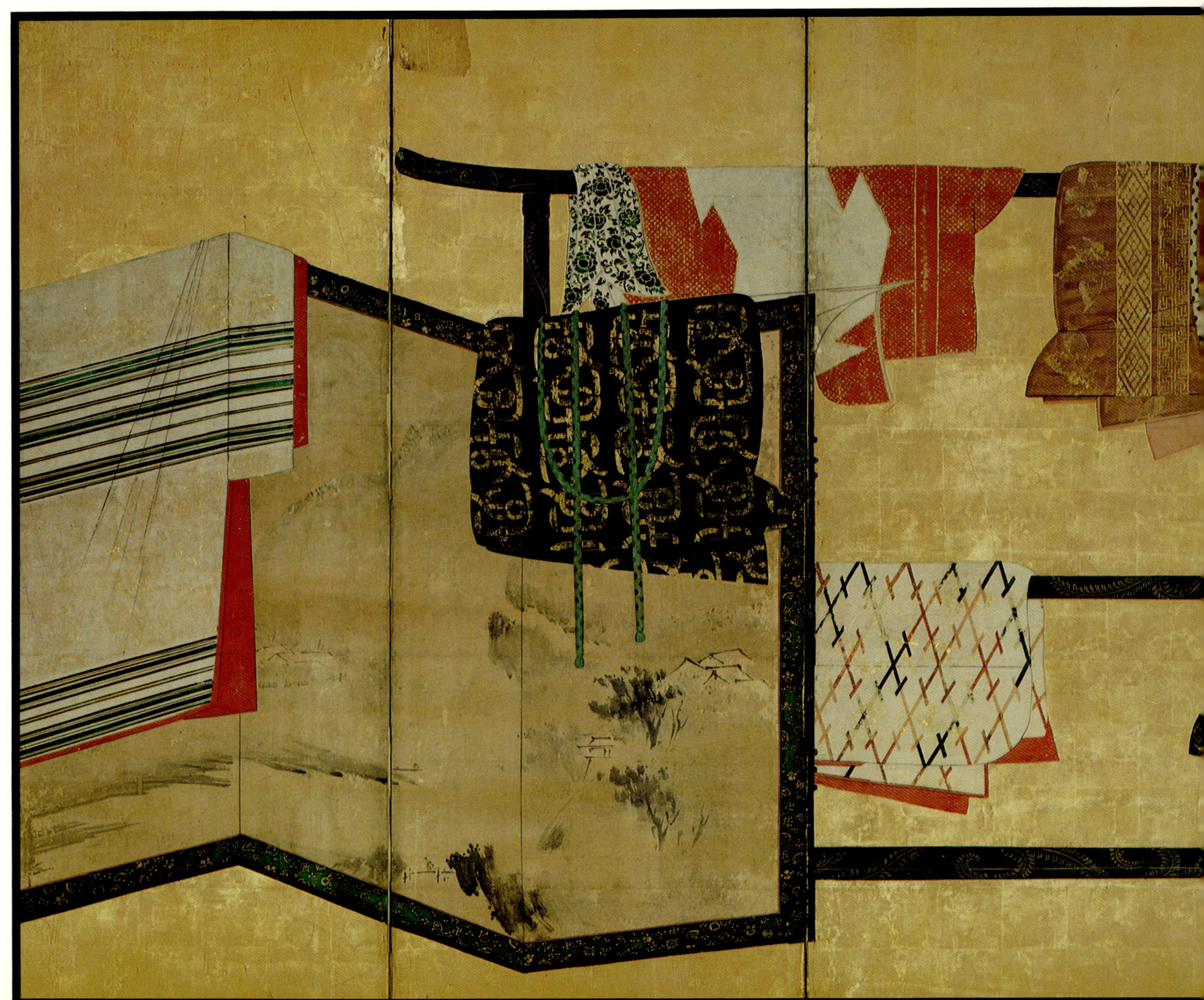

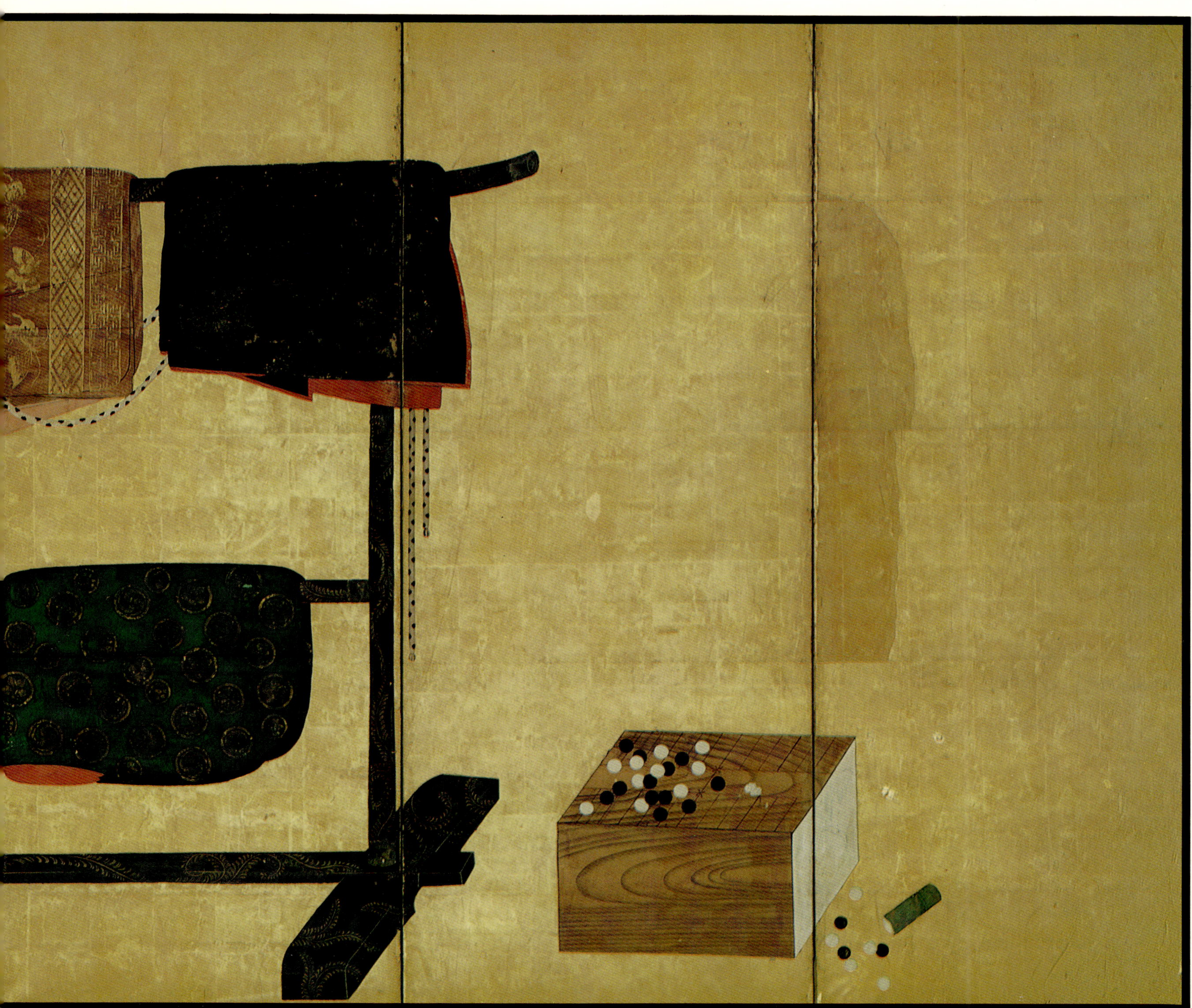

**9.
Tagasode**
Left screen

9.
TAGASODE (Whose Sleeves…)
Edo period, seventeenth century
Pair of six-fold screens; color and gold on paper
172 cm. x 384 cm., each

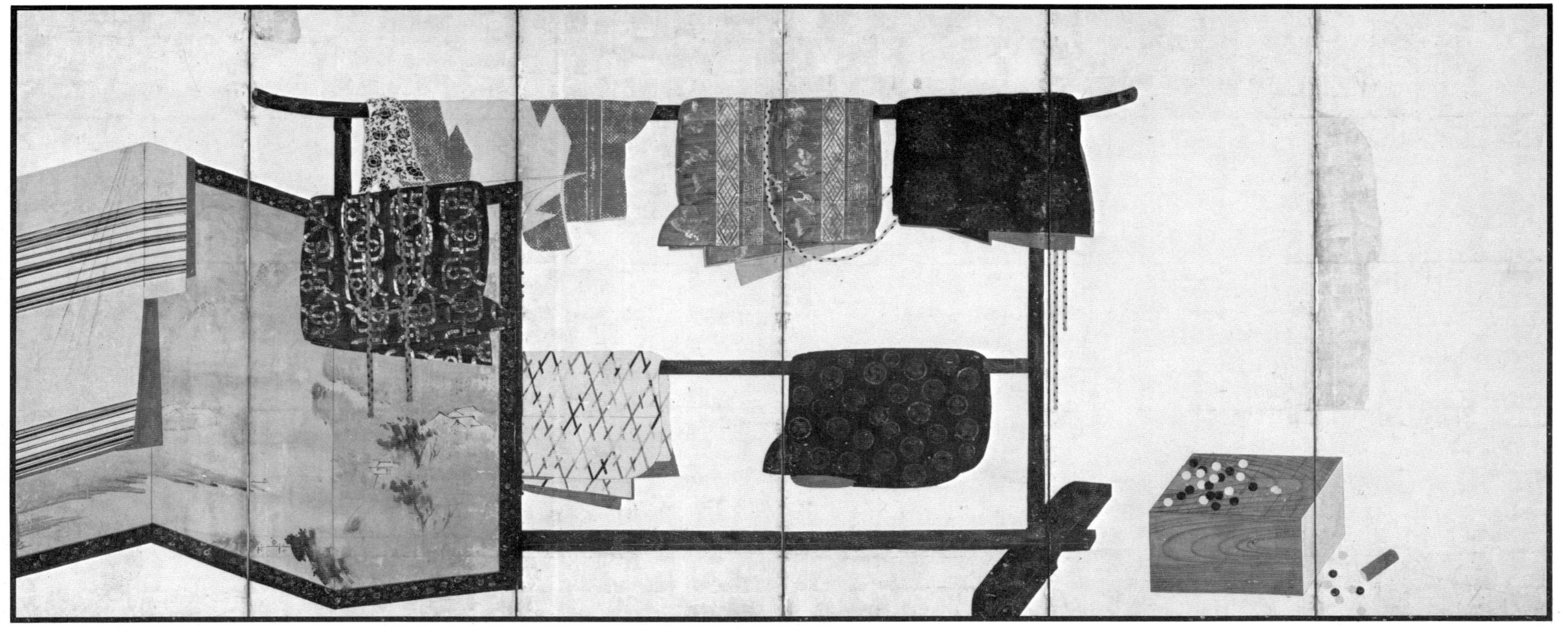

The genre paintings of Japan's "early modern" period feature men and women dressed in *kosode* with bold, eye-catching designs. By the Momoyama period the *kosode,* a kimono having narrow hand openings at the ends of the sleeves, had come to be the common outer garment for men and women of all classes. The use of this garment, which was the model for the present day kimono, accompanied the rise of the Nō drama in Japan. The Momoyama period saw a rapid development in textile manufacture, and new decorative techniques and patterns were devised for the fabrics used in making both *kosode* and Nō robes.

This trend in fashion is the background for the appearance of the Tagasode screen. *Tagasode* (Whose Sleeves. . .) is a word that appears frequently in the classical Japanese poetry of the late Heian and Kamakura periods. The screens were given this name because the garments that appear in the paintings, casually draped over a kimono rack, were evocative of the woman who wore these stylish patterns.

In the right screen of this pair, the *kosode* robe with the gold pattern of wisteria blossoms on clouds resembles a Nō robe, and the decorated box to the right of the rack appears to be a box for Nō masks. A similar rack is in the center of the left screen with a *sugoroku* (Japanese backgammon) board placed to the right. Both the kimono rack and the screen to the left are draped with elegant robes. The free, rapidly brushed ink landscape that appears on the screen gives us some idea of the extent of this anonymous artist's ability.

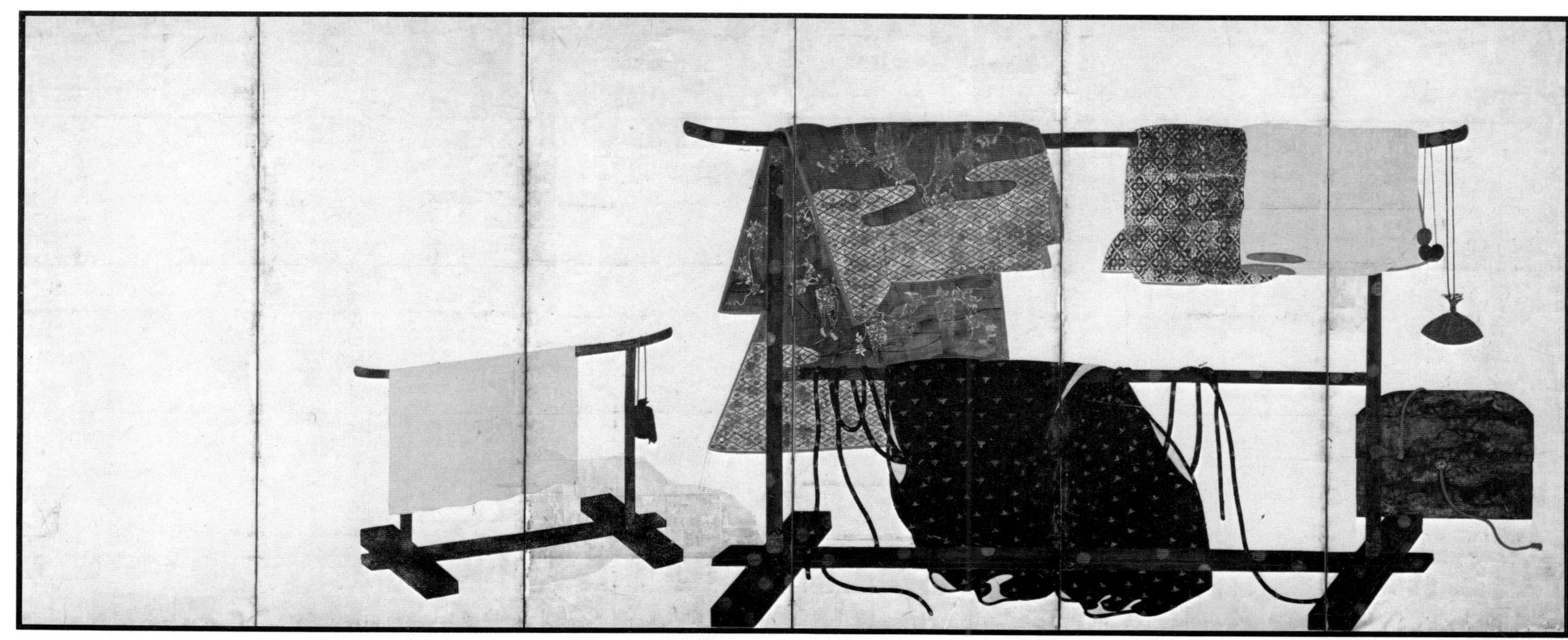

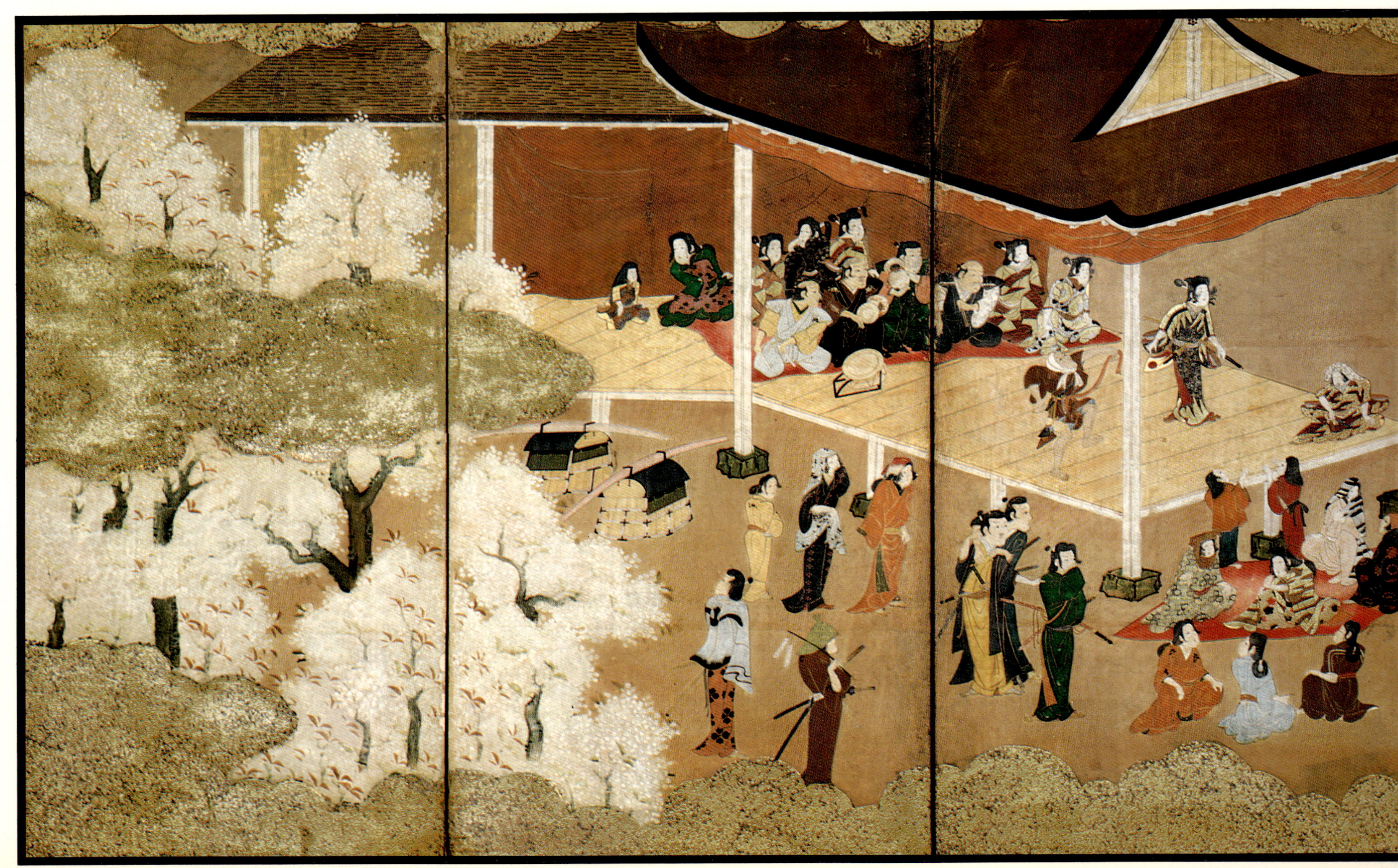

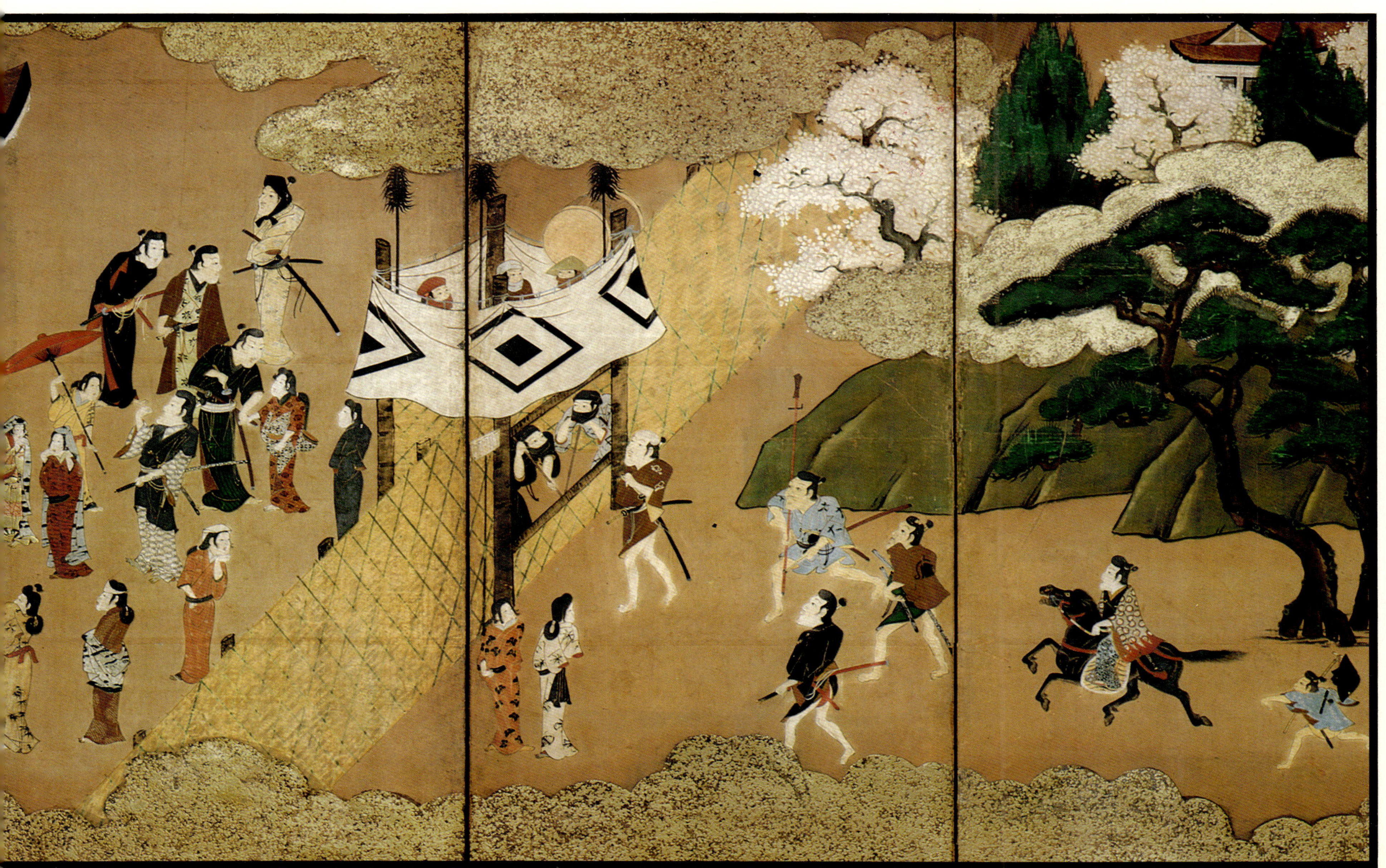

10.
OKUNI KABUKI
Edo period, seventeenth century
Six-fold screen; color and gold on paper
133 cm. x 365.7 cm.

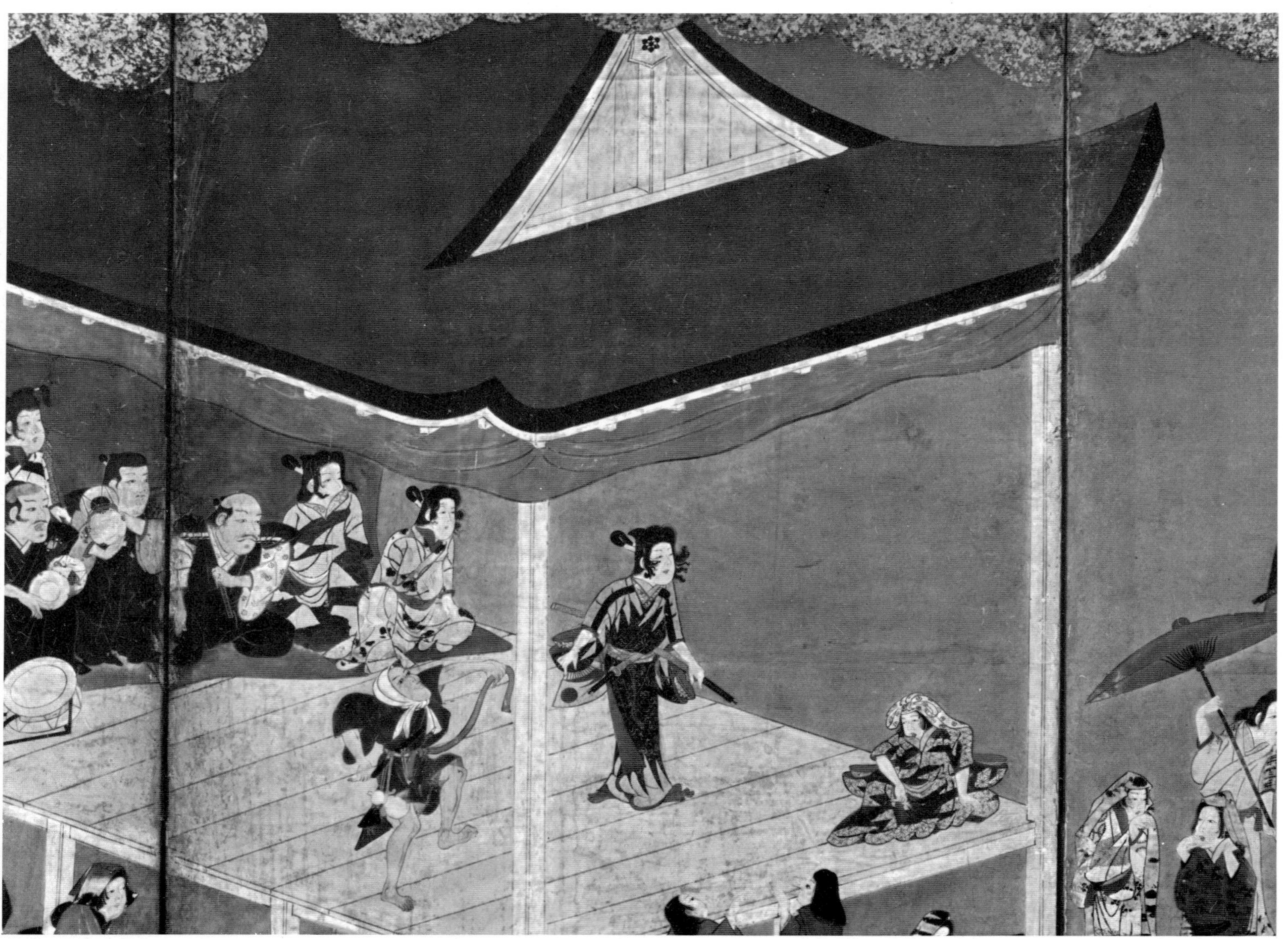

Kabuki, one of Japan's most popular theatre arts originated in the late Momoyama period and developed into its present form during the Edo period. A woman named Okuni is considered the originator of Kabuki as a form of dance entertainment, and depictions of her in a theatre performance are a common subject on genre screens and scrolls. Okuni is said to have been a *miko,* or shrine maiden, in the service of Izumo Taisha, the great Shinto shrine located in Shimane Prefecture. It is recorded that she appeared in Kyoto in the early years of the seventeenth century and established a stage near the Kitano Shrine (See No. 1). There she performed the *nembutsu odori,* a ritual prayer dance that invokes the name of Amida Buddha, interspersed with popular dances, songs, and skits. It is apparent from paintings that this *"Kabuki odori,"* as Okuni's per-formance came to be called, became a very popular dance entertainment among the citizens of Kyoto.

This screen shows a relaxed and amused audience watching a performance of *"Kabuki odori"* in progress. The scene depicted is one of the principal acts of the skit in which Okuni, the central figure dressed as a man, uses a comic character (*saruwaka*) on the left to make advances to a teahouse madam who is cowering at the corner of the stage on the right. Seated at the back of the stage are musicians who play flutes and drums. In Okuni's time the musical accompaniment was the same as that used for Nō plays. The *samisen,* which became a standard musical instrument in later Kabuki performances, was not yet in general use.

The *Okuni Kabuki* was so successful that the same type of song and dance entertainment was imitated by the *yūjo,* or courtesans of Kyoto. Commonly called *Onna Kabuki* (Female Kabuki), it flourished for a time in the entertainment district of Shijō-Kawaramachi but was banned in 1629 because of its detrimental effects on public morals. [8]

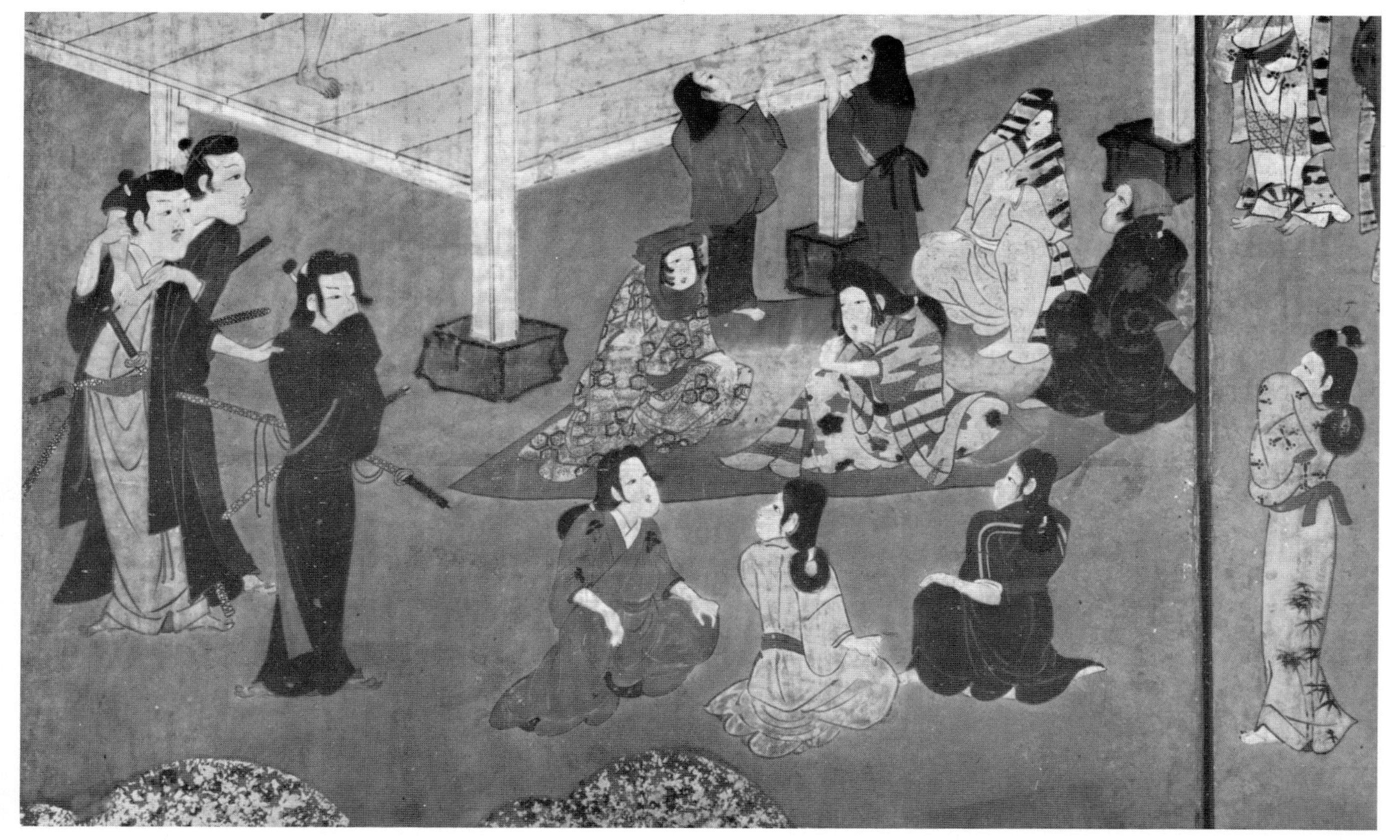

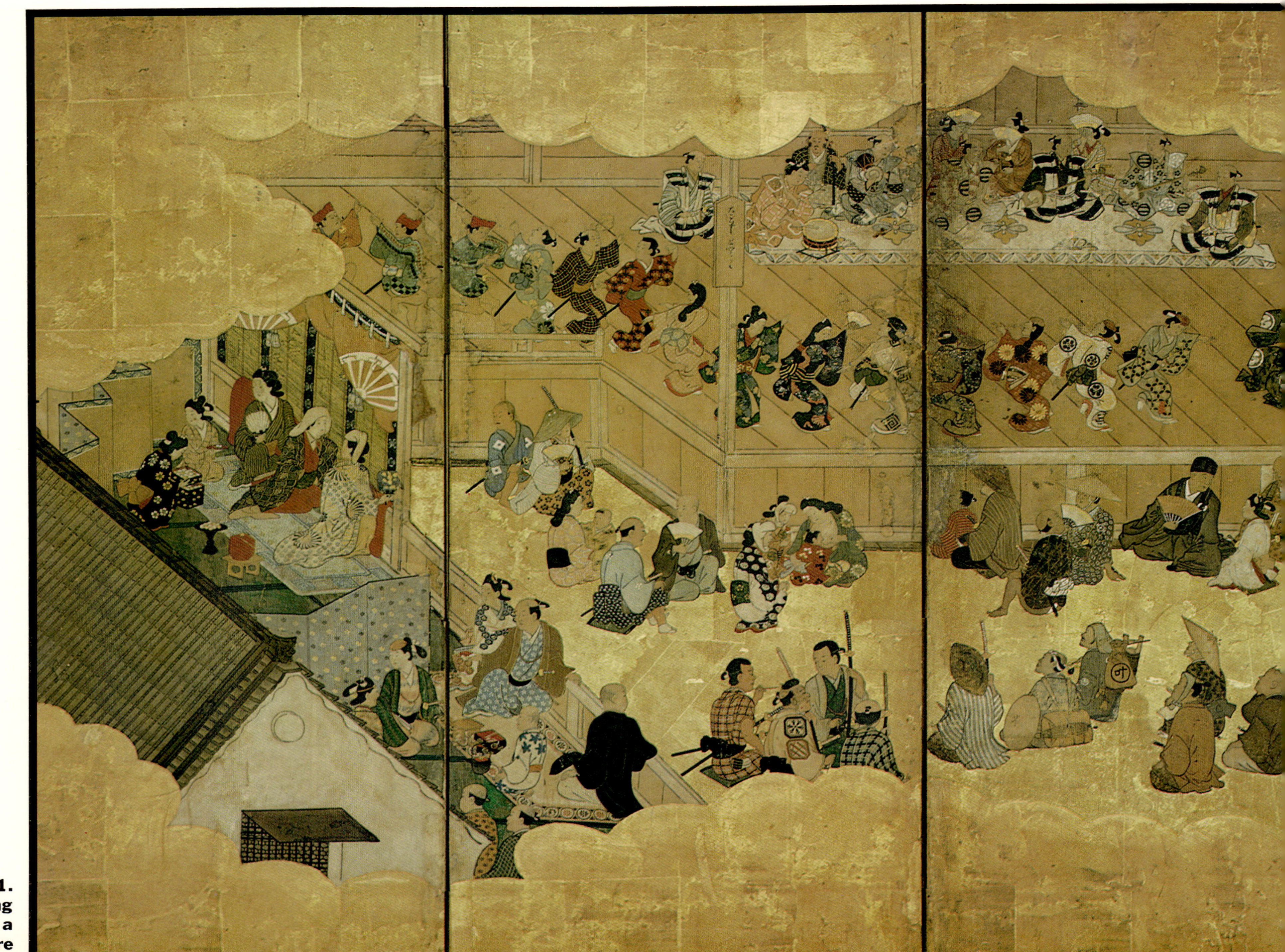

**11.
Flower Viewing
at Ueno and a
Kabuki Theatre**
Right screen

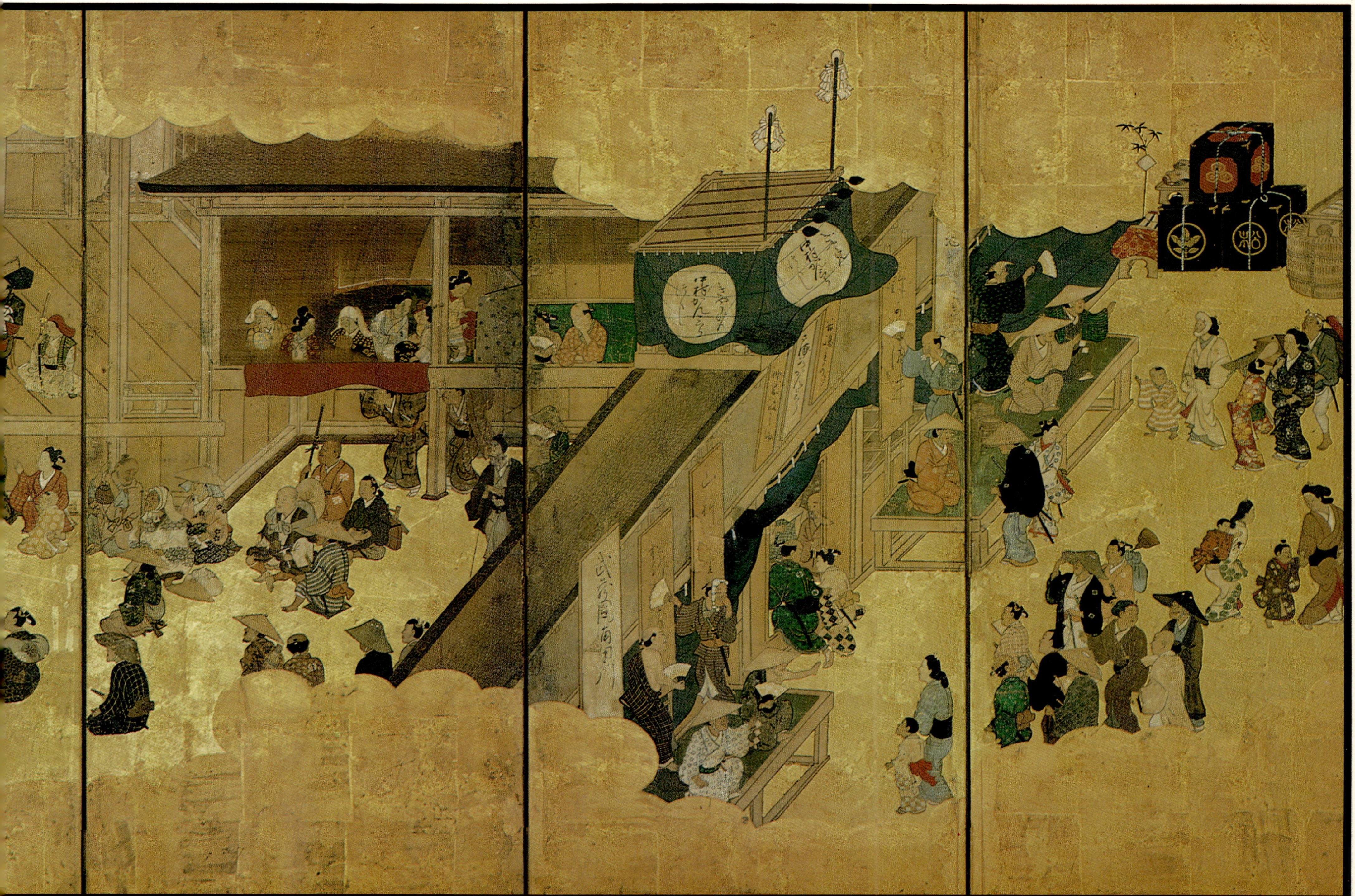

11.
FLOWER VIEWING AT UENO AND A KABUKI THEATRE
Edo period
Attributed to Hishikawa Moronobu (1618–94)
Pair of six-fold screens; color and gold on paper
95.7 cm. 234.4 cm., each

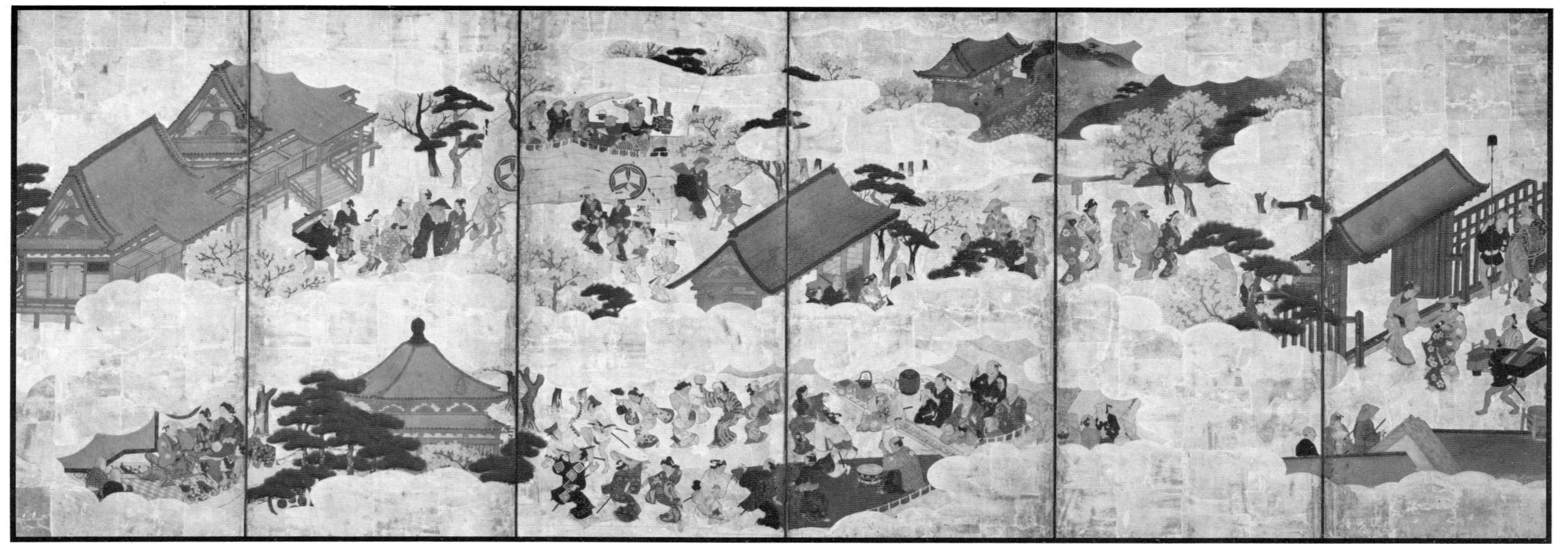

The genre painting that flourished from the Momoyama period to the early part of the long Edo period used themes drawn from the life and landscape of the ancient capital of Kyoto. However, when the cultural initiative in Japan shifted from Kyoto to the new capital, Edo (modern Tokyo), after the middle of the seventeenth century, artists lost sight of the original focus of genre painting. The merchants of Edo, a group of *nouveau riche* consumers, made *ukiyo-e* the idol of their artistic interests. Since the spirit of "early modern" genre painting flowed within its themes, *ukiyo-e* was not something that developed by itself as an artistic style separate from genre painting. Instead *ukiyo-e* gradually evolved out of a basic orientation towards the depiction of figures and genre activity.

Hishikawa Moronobu is credited with crystalizing a new *ukiyo-e* style within the context of the early genre painting formulas. He had studied the classical techniques of the Tosa and Kanō schools as well as genre painting. He was the first artist to design single-sheet woodblock prints, thereby raising the woodblock to the level of an independent work of art.

The left screen of this pair shows groups of people enjoying flower viewing at Ueno, a section of Edo that was famous for cherry blossoms. The right screen depicts actors and spectators at a performance of a play at a theatre called the Nakamura-za, active during the Genroku era (1688–1705). Kabuki as a theatre art developed rapidly from about the middle of the seventeenth century, and everything about it, including the length of the stage, became larger and more grand. The name of the actor, Nakamura Kanzaburō, a popular and highly acclaimed actor of the day, appears on the curtain that covers the wooden scaffolding of the theatre gate.[9]

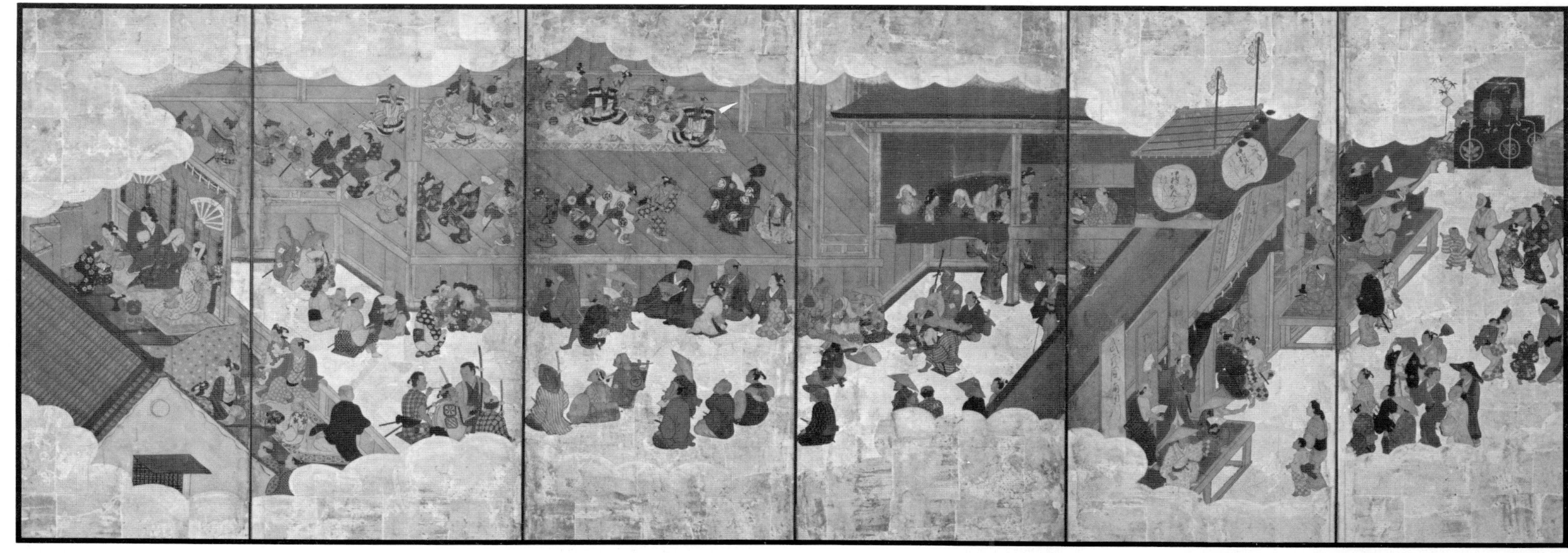

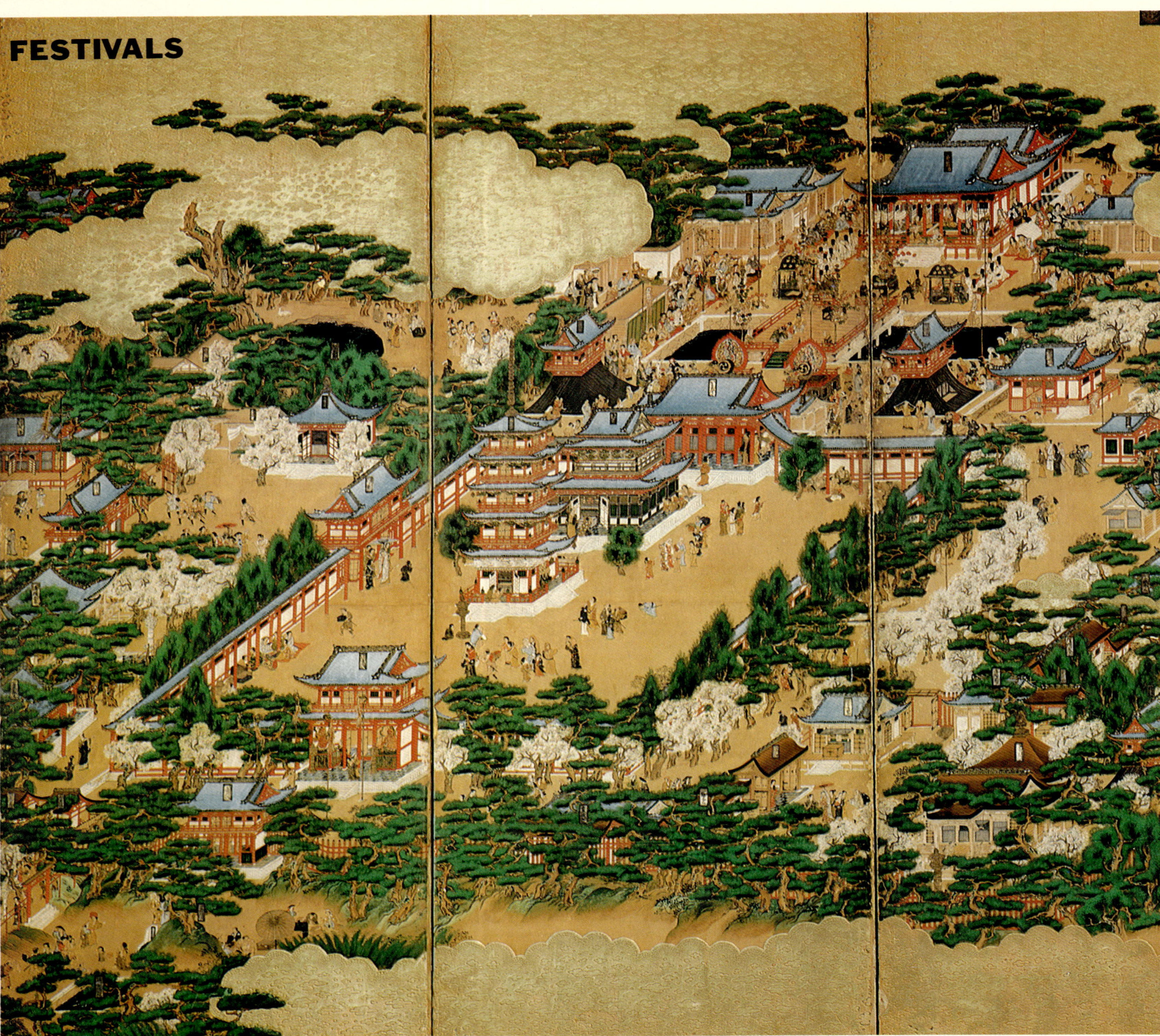

12.
Festivals of
Shitennō-ji and
Sumiyoshi Shrine
Detail right screen

12.
Festivals
of Shitennō-ji and
Sumiyoshi Shrine
Detail left screen

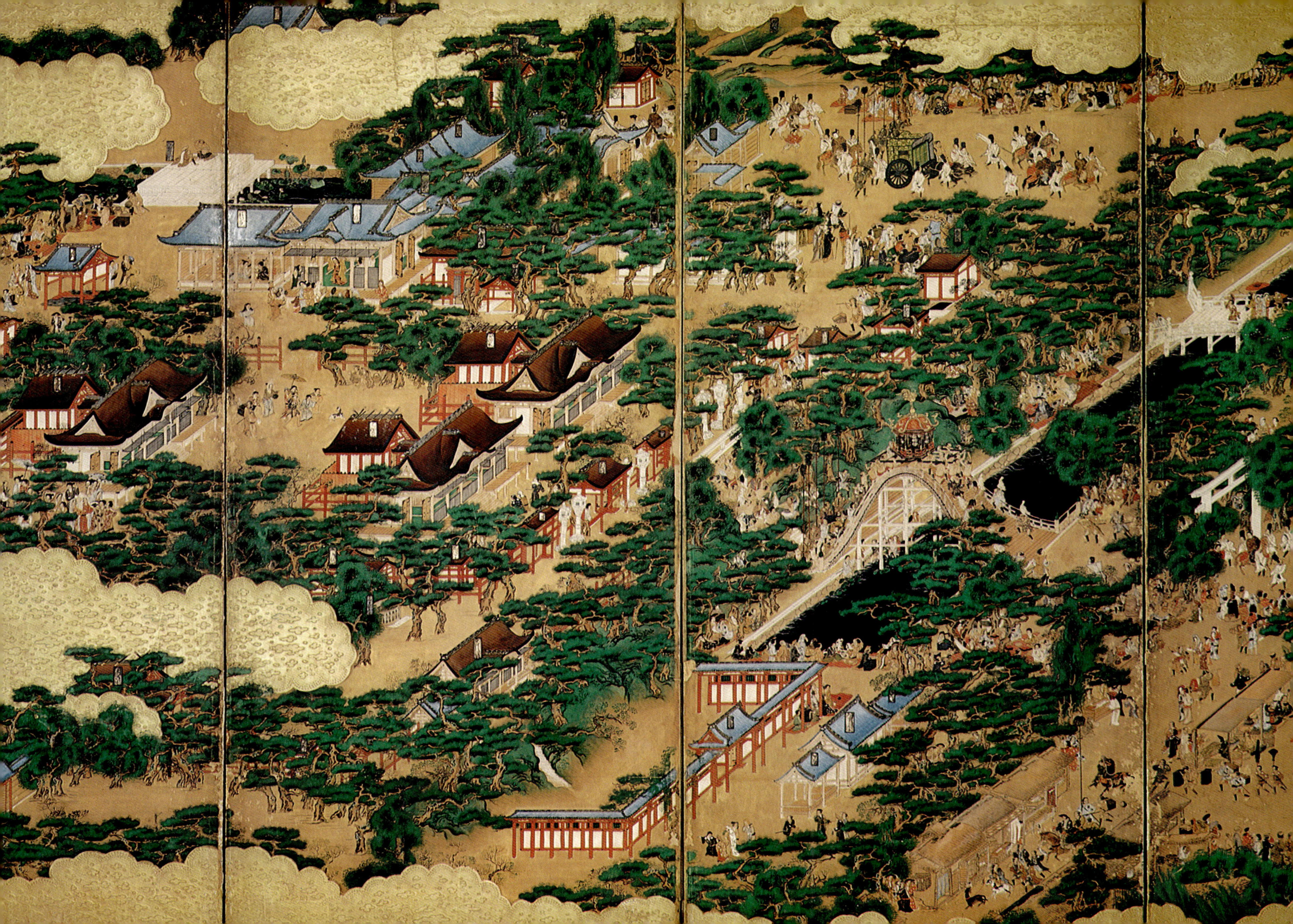

12.
FESTIVALS OF SHITENNŌ-JI AND SUMIYOSHI SHRINE
Edo period, seventeenth century
Pair of six-fold screens; color and gold on paper
168 cm. x 382.8 cm., each

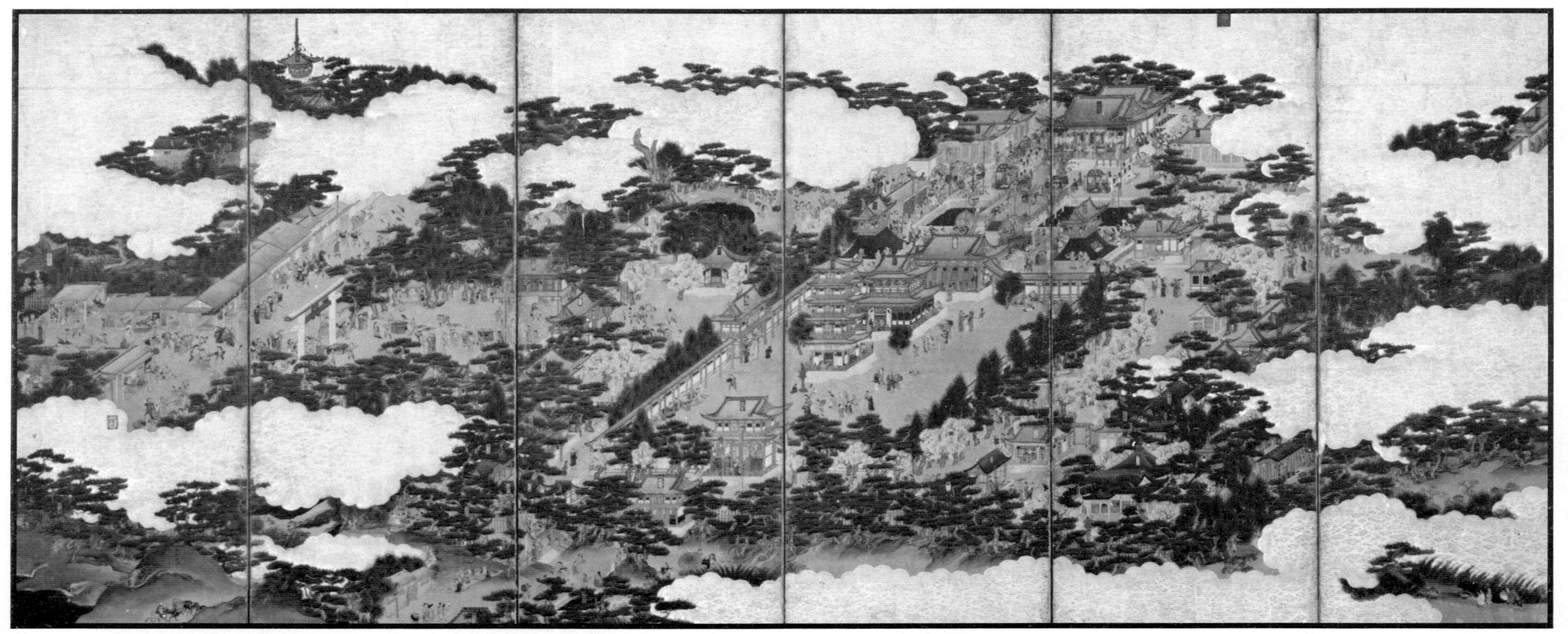

Buddhist temple and Shinto shrine festivals flourished during the late Momoyama and early Edo periods. Since they were large, colorful affairs, attended by people from various classes of society, festivals became a favored topic of genre painting. This screen pair is an unusual set of paintings showing the major festivals at the Shitennō-ji temple and the Sumiyoshi Shrine, both located in Osaka. The respective temple and shrine complexes are depicted with great accuracy in splendid overviews, and all activities of the booming festivals are faithfully described.

The festival shown on the Shitennō-ji screen is the *Shōryōe* which is held annually on the twenty-second day of May. The *Shōryōe* is a Buddhist memorial service that commemorates the memory of Prince Shōtoku, the founder of Shitennō-ji. The twenty-second day of May (by the lunar calendar, the twenty-second day of the second month) was established as the festival day because Prince Shōtoku died on that day. This painting records one of the major events of the festival, the *Bugaku* dance that takes place in front of the Rokuji-dō, located behind the main Shitennō-ji compound.

The festival depicted on the right screen at the Sumiyoshi Shrine is an annual summer event which occurs on the first day of August. The *kami,* or Shinto gods, enshrined at Sumiyoshi include protective deities for ships and sailors as well as the patron deity of *waka* poetry. One of the highlights of the festival depicted here is the transport of a shrine cart *(mikoshi)* weighing 1850 kilos to the shrine precincts. In this dramatic scene, shipowners shoulder the cart to carry it over the high arched bridge to the shrine.

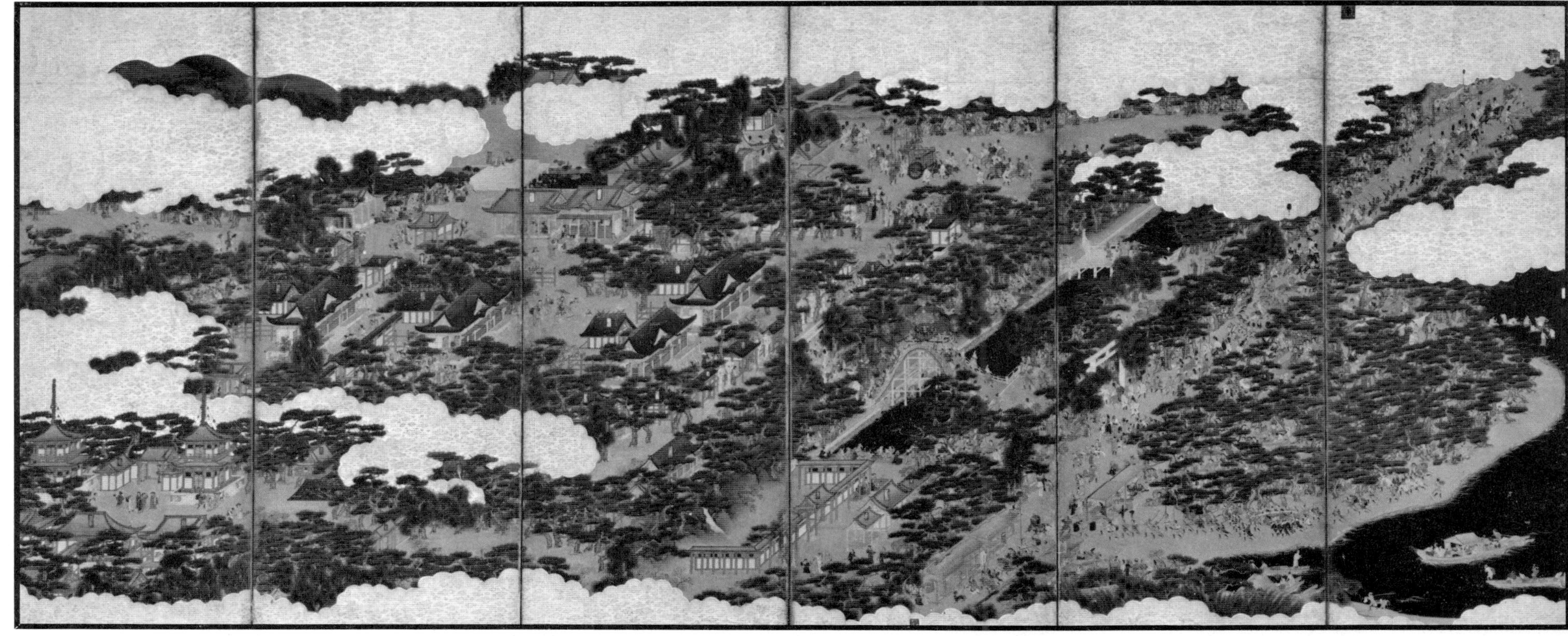

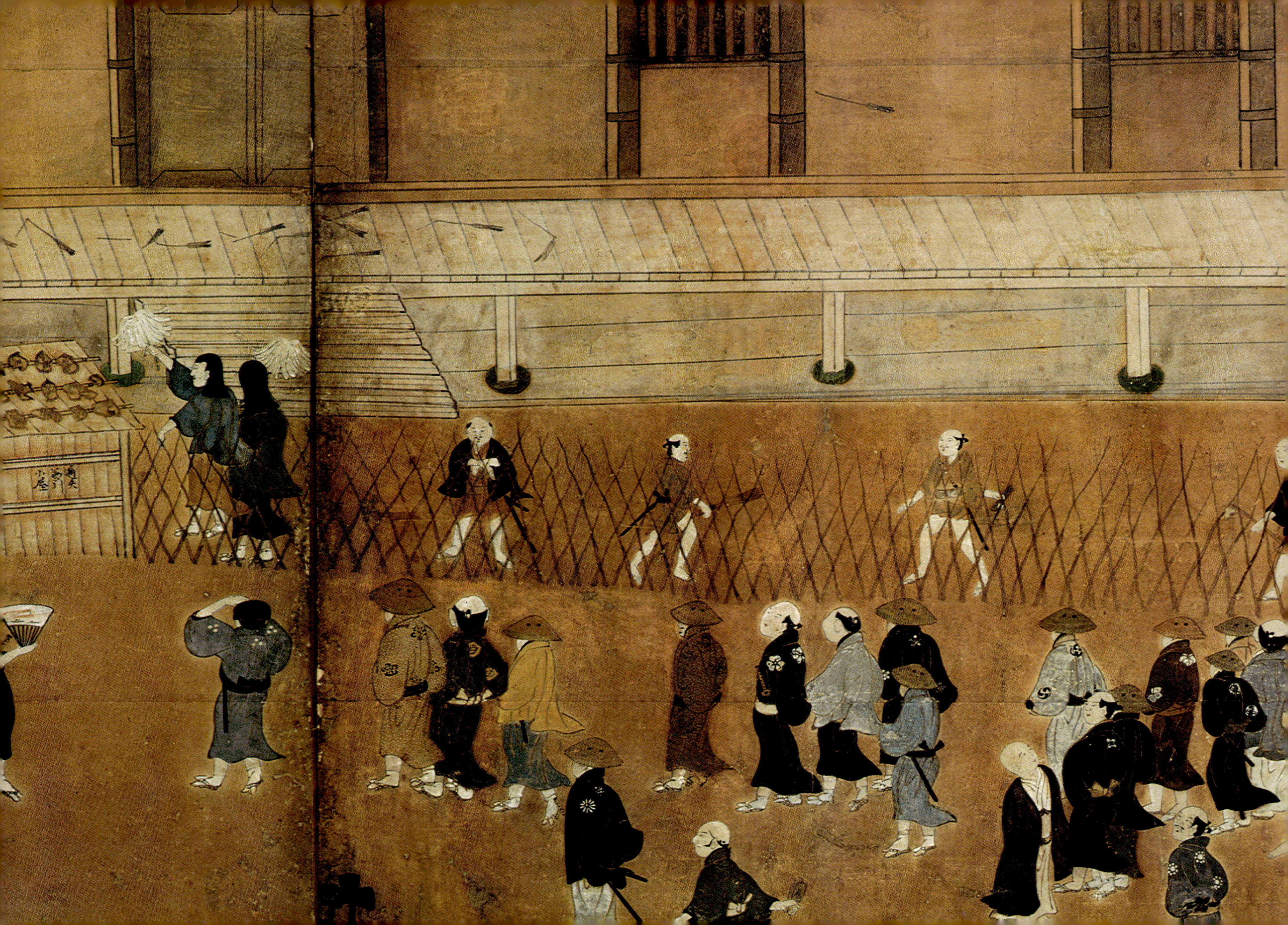
矢
屋

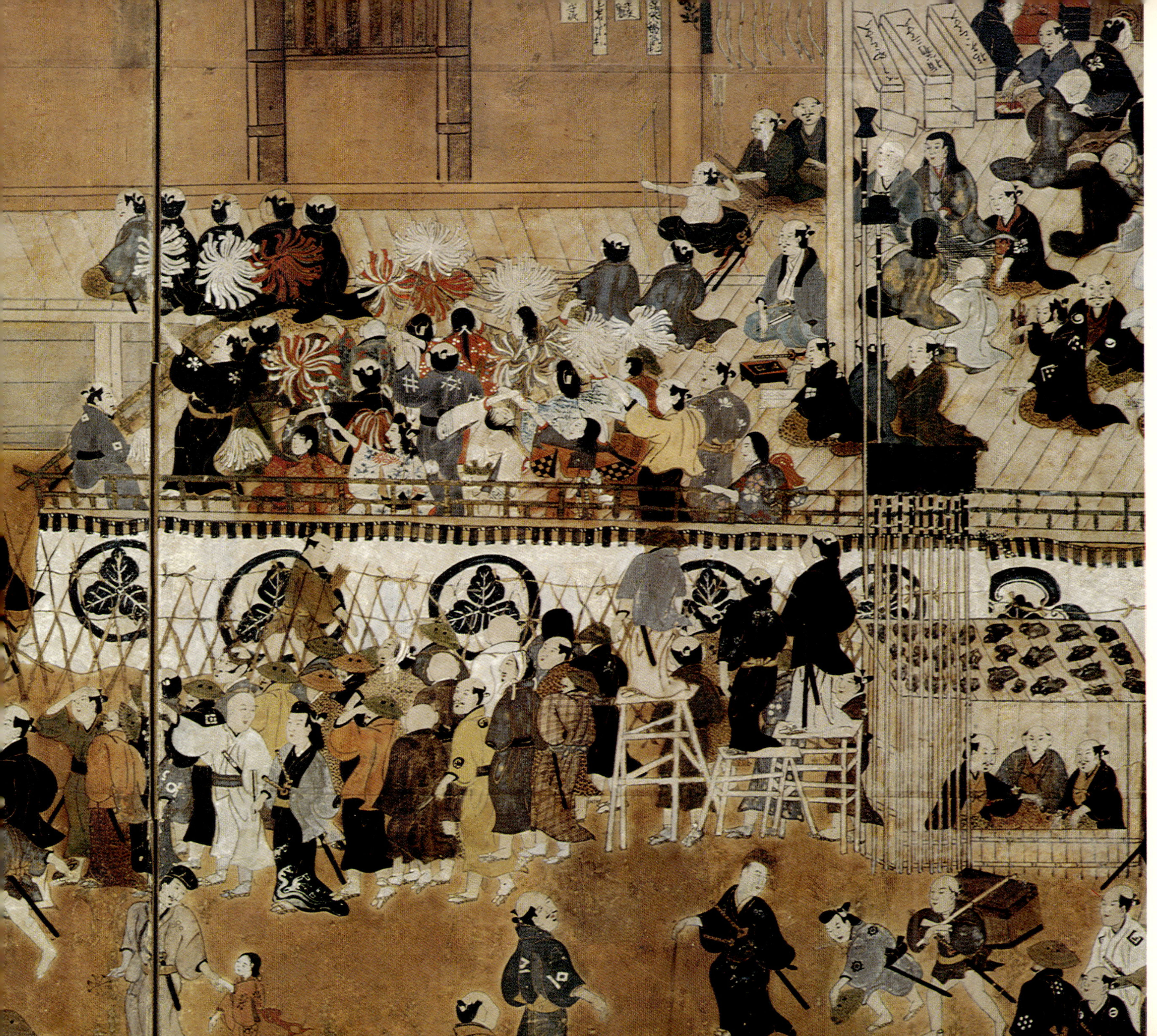

13.
Archery Contest at
Sanjūsangen-dō
Detail

13.
ARCHERY CONTEST AT SANJŪSANGEN-DŌ
Edo period, seventeenth century
Six-fold screen; color on paper
89.1 cm. x 360.6 cm.

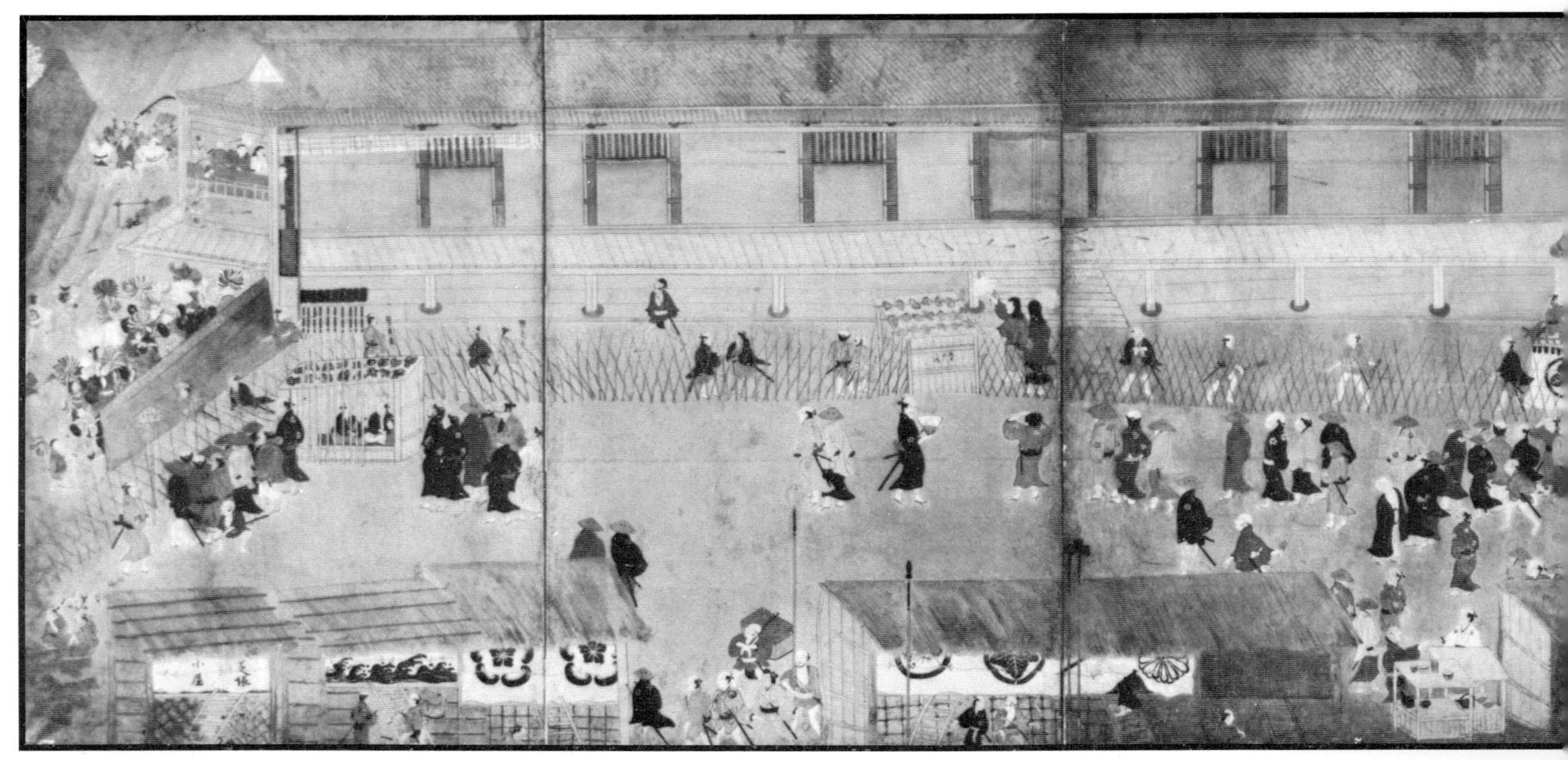

The Rengeō-in, a temple located in the Higashiyama section of Kyoto, is better known by its popular name, Sanjūsangen-dō, or the Temple of Thirty-three Bays. A bay is an architectural unit defined by the space between the pillars basic to the temple construction. Sanjūsangen-dō is dedicated to the One Thousand-Armed Kannon Bodhisattva, and the number of bays used in this temple are symbolic of the thirty-three separate forms of this deity. Because of the unusual number of bays, this temple is very long, measuring just over one hundred eighteen meters. Probably for this reason Sanjūsangen-dō became famous as the site of a great archery contest during the Momoyama period.

The western (back) side of the temple, which has a long, uninterrupted veranda, is used for the contest. The archer is seated at the southern (right) end, and he aims for a target placed at the northern end of the temple. The archer must aim carefully to avoid sending arrows into the eaves, the sides, or the veranda of the building. Each archer takes his place at six o'clock in the evening and shoots continuously over a period of twenty-four hours. The contest is determined by the participant having the largest number of arrows to reach the target. The record-holders thus far are one Hoshi no Kanzaemon, a vassal of the domain of Owari (now part of Aichi Prefecture), who is credited with 8,000 hits in 1669, and Wasa Daihachi, a warrior from the domain of Kii (present day Wakayama Prefecture), who sent 8,133 arrows to the mark in 1687.

In this painting the temple extends across the upper left. A bamboo fence encloses the western lawn, and a platform was constructed for participants and officials at the southern end. The archer notches arrow after arrow, and a number can be seen flying towards the target at the extreme left. The archery contest took on the character of a major festival event in the Momoyama and early Edo periods. Crowds gathered, food stalls were opened, and spectators raised their voices with shouts of approval when an arrow struck the target. [10]

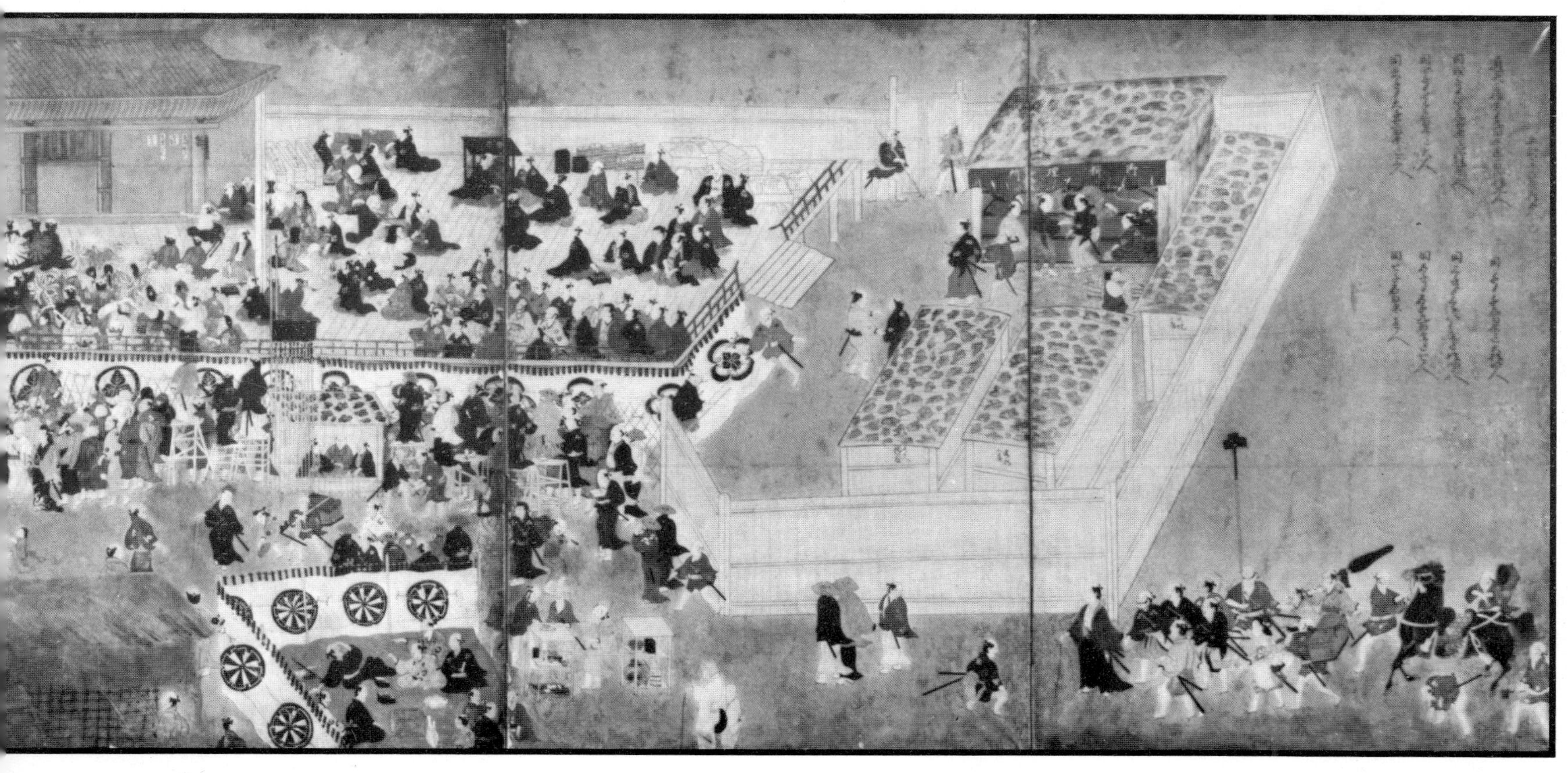

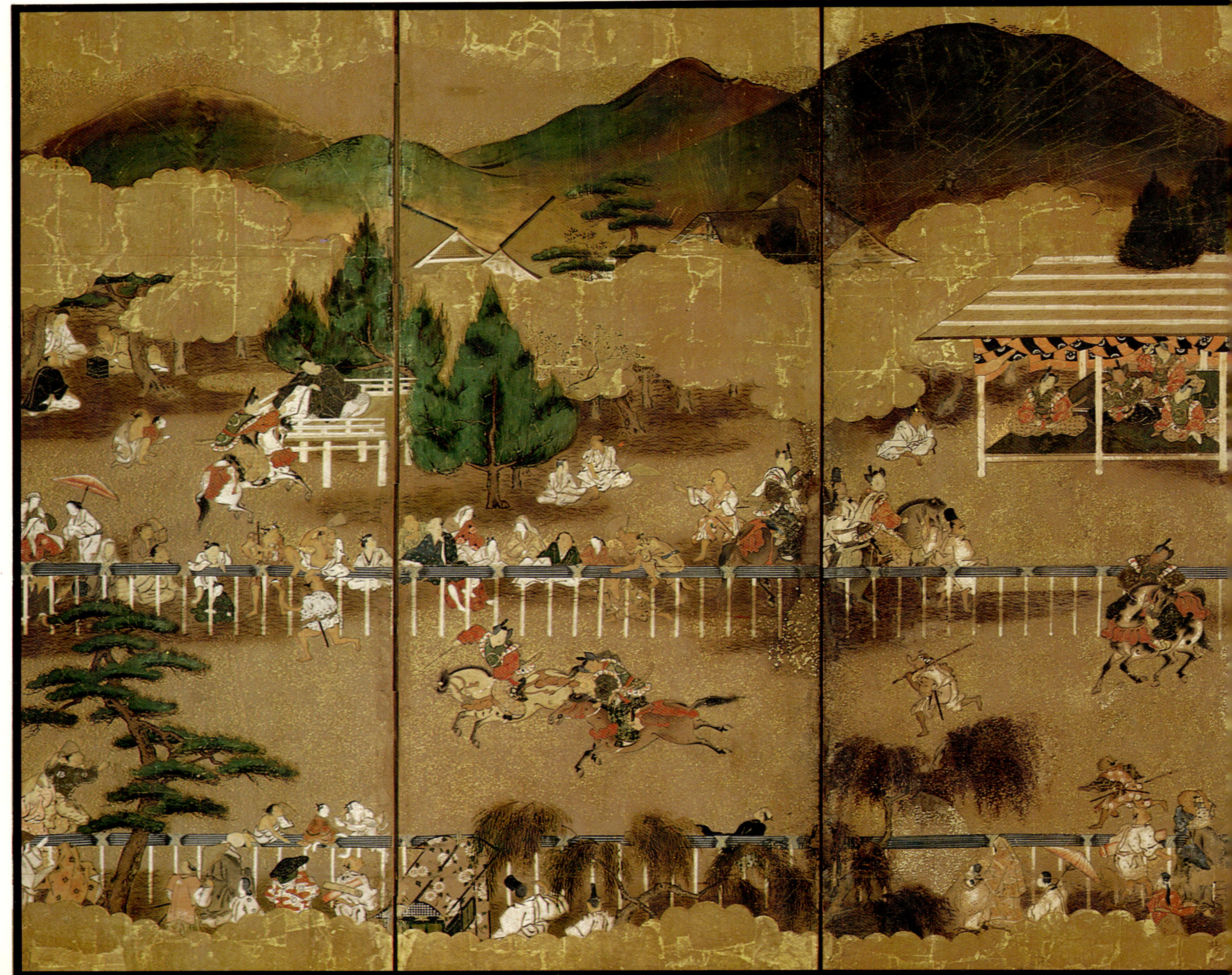

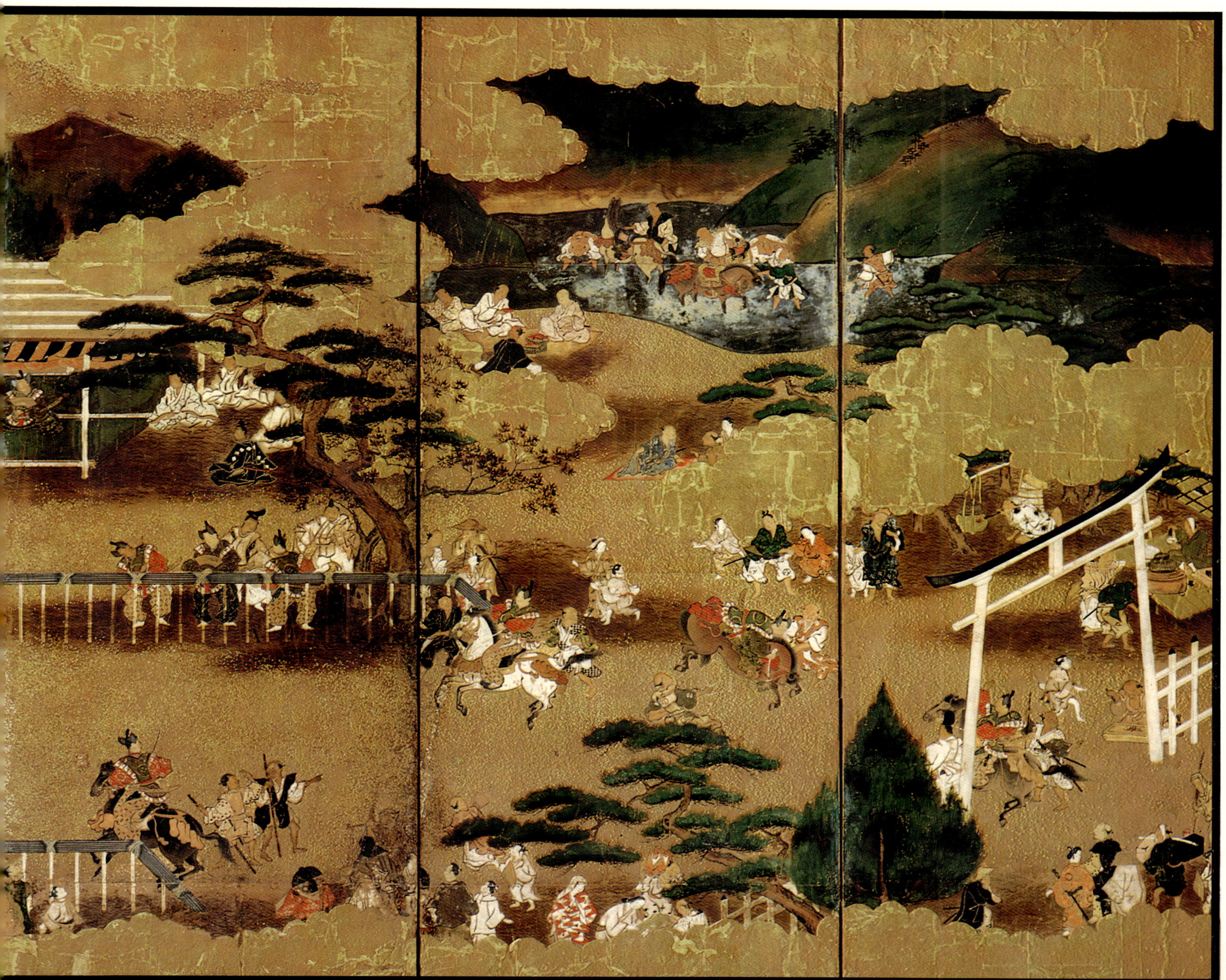

**14.
Horse Races
at Kamo**
Right screen

14.

HORSE RACES AT KAMO
Edo period, eighteenth century
Pair of six-fold screens; color and gold on paper
120 cm. x 275 cm., each

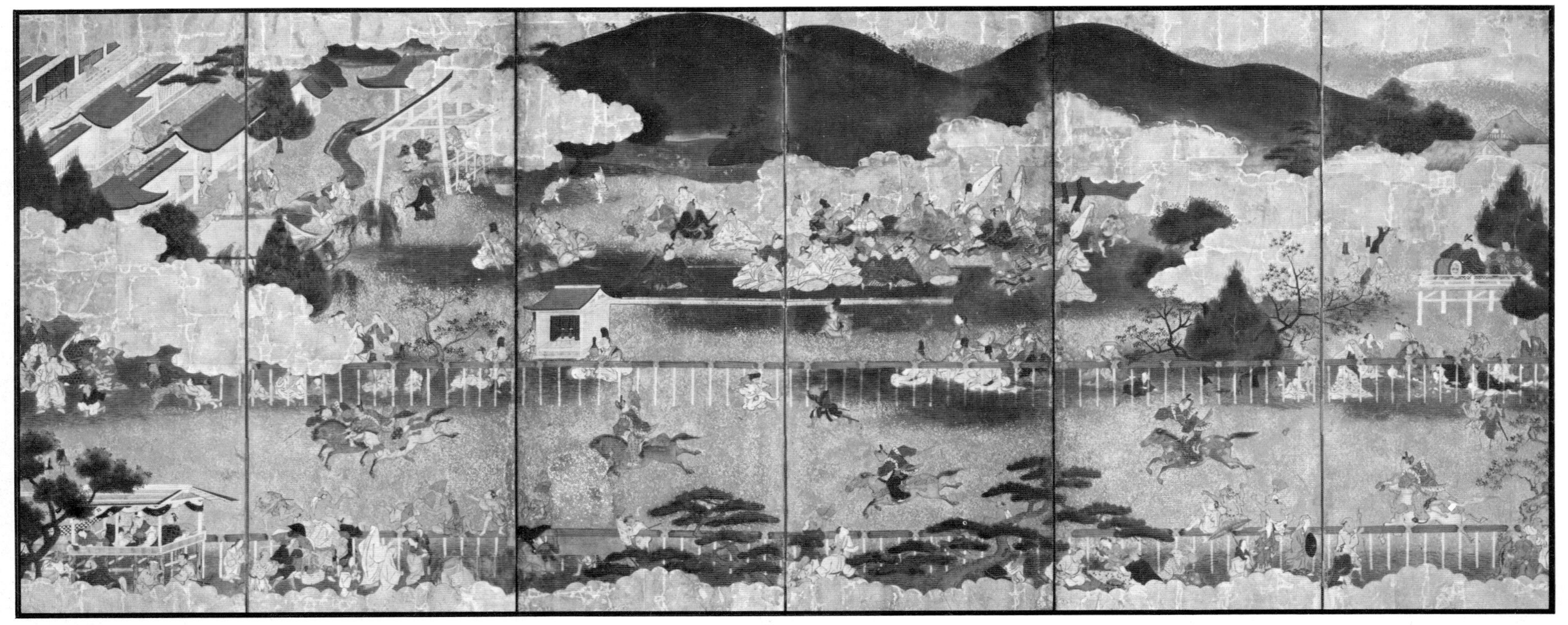

The horse races at the Kamigamo Shrine in Kyoto are an annual event that takes place on the fifth of May. Since public interest in this contest was strong in the late Momoyama and early Edo periods, it became a popular subject of genre painting as a festival event. This pair of screens is a realistic depiction of the famous races.

The Kamo race track, which is delineated by parallel fences, is a straight course set between the two *torii* (sacred gates) of the shrine. In this screen pair the first *torii* where the race begins is visible in the first panel of the right screen, and the track extends from right to left across the surface of both screens. Visible in the upper left corner of the left screen is a portion of the main shrine precinct showing the second *torii* and a portion of the garden through which flows the Mitarashi River where worshippers wash their hands to purify themselves before their visit.

The Kamo horse races are a contest between two teams designated "Right" and "Left," each having ten members. A pair of contestants, one member from each team, race from the starting line marked by the first *torii* to the finish. At the side of the track a temporary shrine is constructed to house the spirit of the shrine deity (*kami*) in whose honor the races are held. This temporary shrine is visible in the fourth panel of the left screen. A shelter for the several umpires who judge the races is also built at the side of the track. If a member of the "Left" team wins, the judges raise a fan marked with a red circle. If the "Right" team wins, a fan with a white circle is raised. The winner is presented with a bolt of white silk.[11]

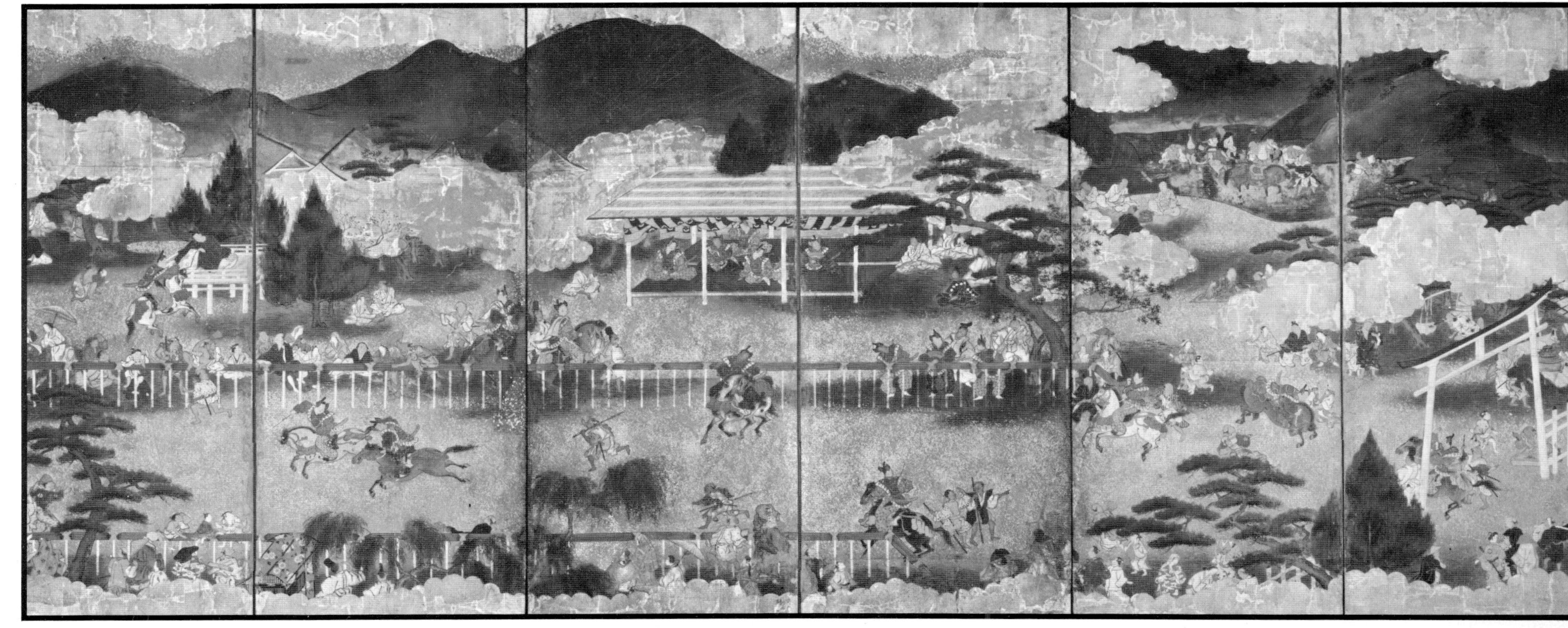

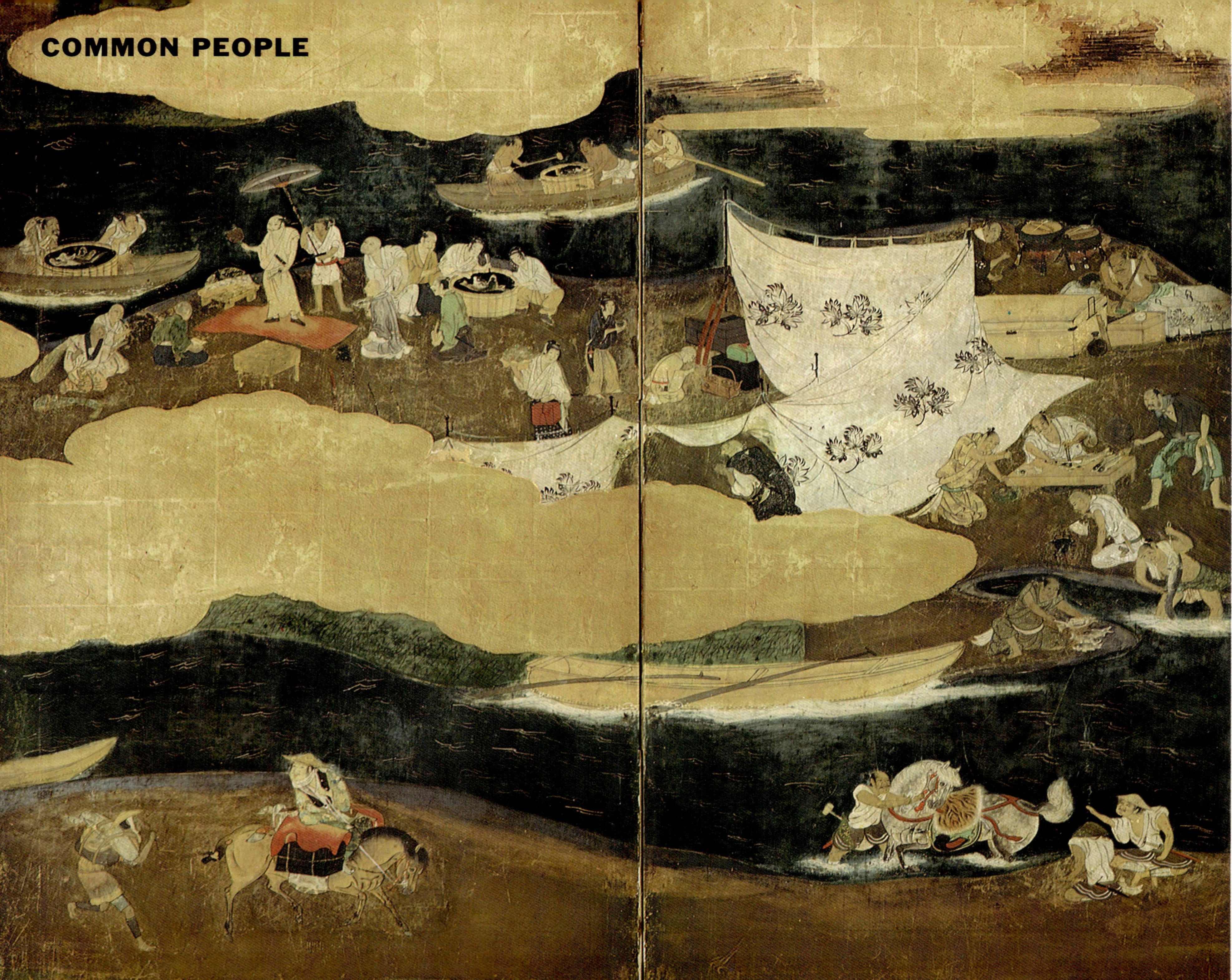

**15.
Fishing Scenes**
Detail left screen

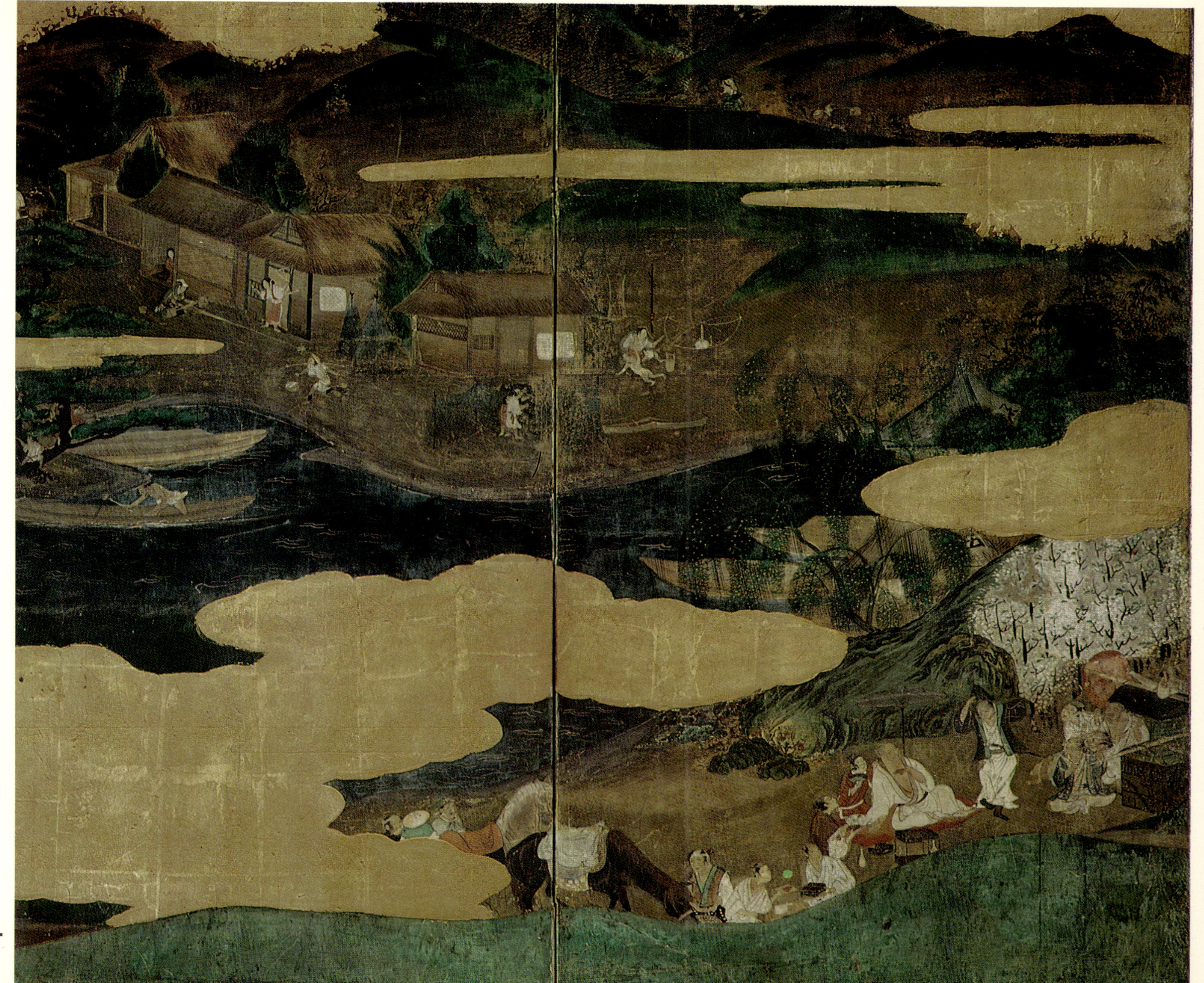

15.
Fishing Scenes
Detail right screen

15.
FISHING SCENES
Edo period, seventeenth century
Pair of six-fold screens; color and gold on paper
169 cm. x 366 cm., each

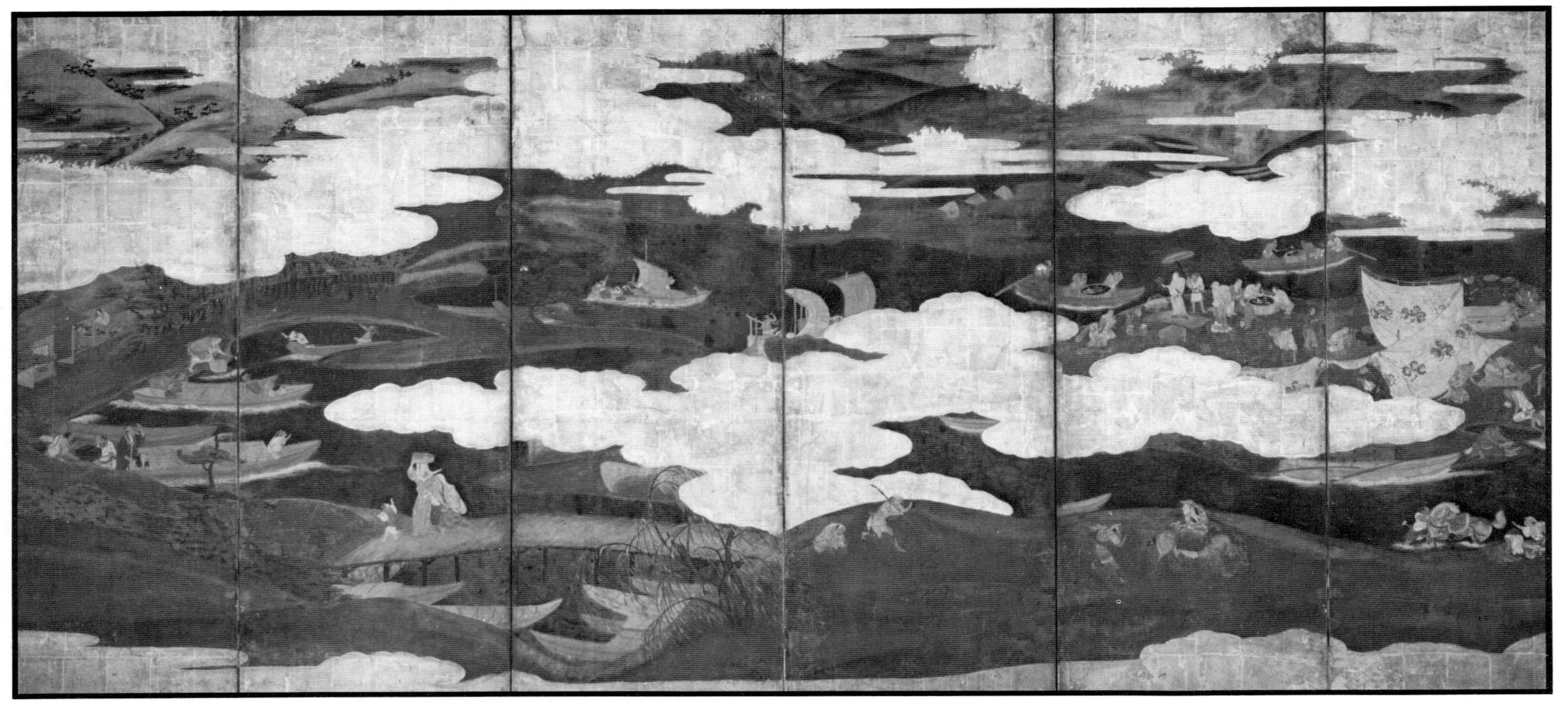

The paintings on this pair of screens, which are separated into pockets by patterns of gold clouds, present a rural landscape situated on the shores of a lake. Although individuals of the noble class are shown enjoying the rustic setting, the principal activity depicted is that of catching fish, as boats ply the waters and fishermen cast their nets. This screen is not believed to have been painted to depict a specific body of water, such as Lake Biwa, but produced as one type of "cultivation pictures" *(kōsaku-zu)* that appeared after the Momoyama period.

Japanese "cultivation pictures" copy the traditional Chinese paintings that take as their subject matter aspects of rural occupations such as farming and weaving. The intent of these paintings is thought to have been more didactic than aesthetic. In this period it was hoped that paintings of common people at work would remind those in government of their responsibilities to the laboring class. Since these themes were common in Chinese style painting, the Tokugawa government gave these commisions to Kanō school painters, for whom the subject was part of the established repertoire.

Genre depictions in the early Edo period looked upon the labors of common people from a number of views. For example, in addition to the general depictions of fishermen and nobleman on an outing in the left screen, the artist took great pains to give a lively expression to a member of the nobleman's party. A male cook carries on an animated conversation with his two companions as he kneels before a large chopping block preparing a fish for his lord. Other paintings exist, however, in which neither didactic qualities nor common work is emphasized. For example, the well-known screen called "Weavers" in the Atami Art Museum in Shizuoka Prefecture is a painting that makes the depiction of ladies in a genre setting more important than their work. The large figures of women at the loom and at sewing are intended to be appreciated more for their beauty than for the fact of their labors.[12]

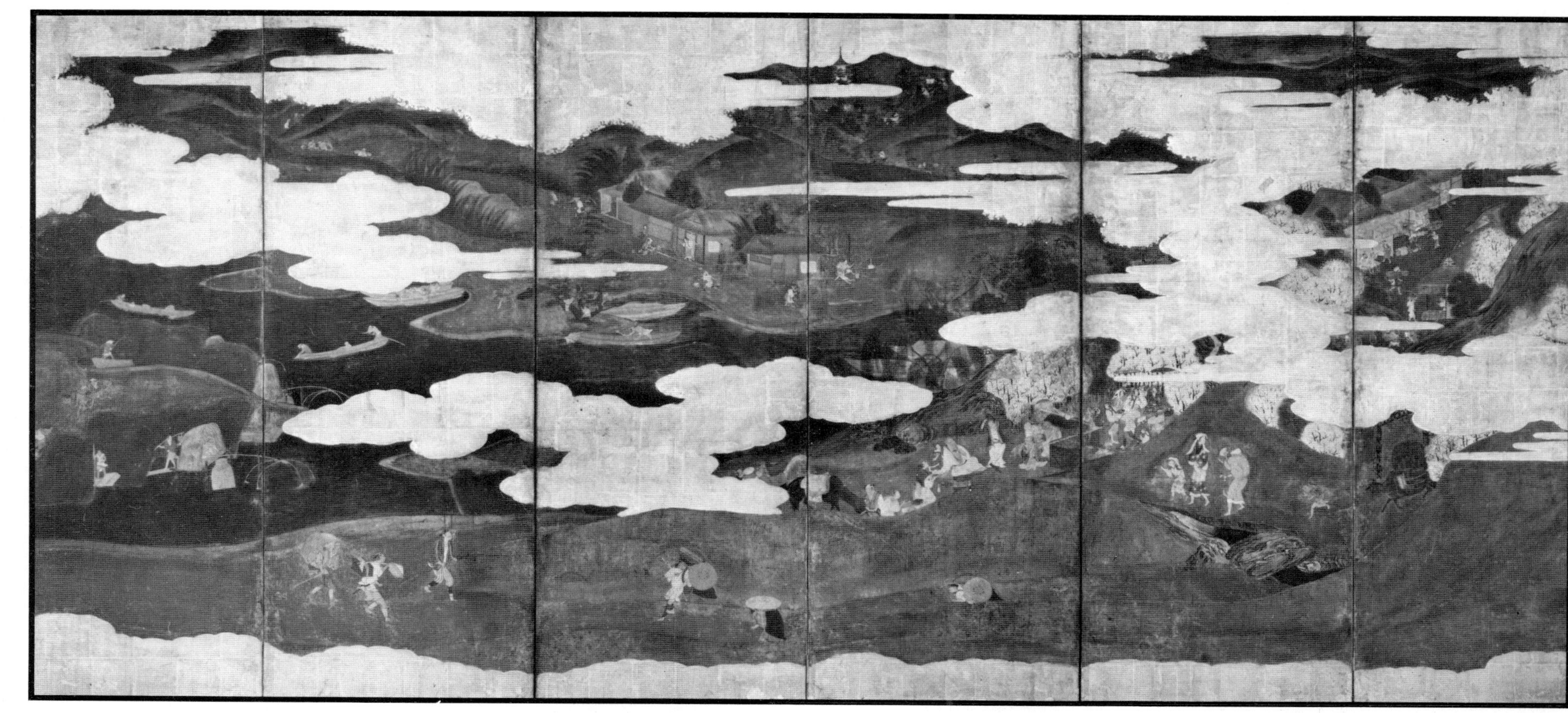

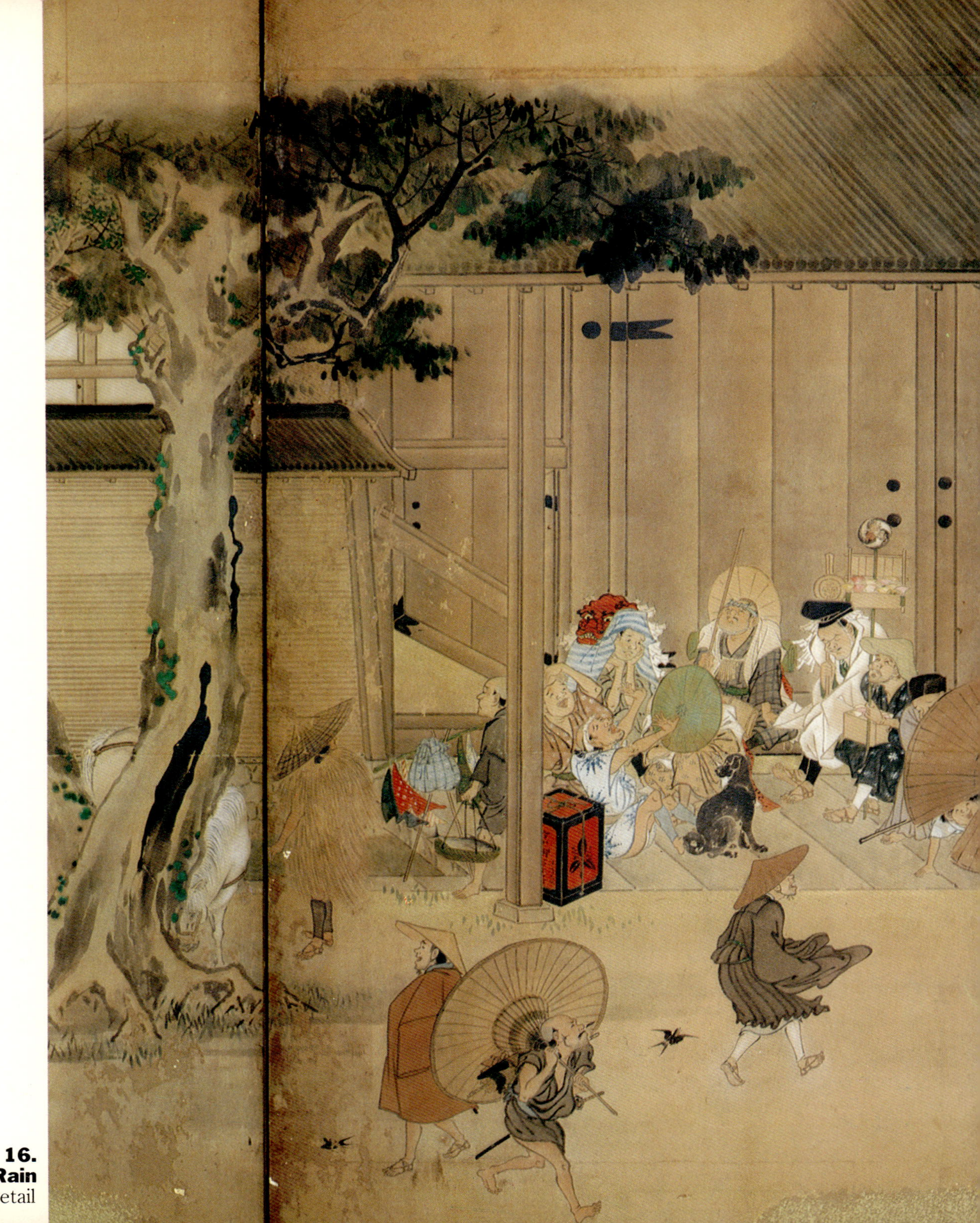

16.
Taking Shelter from the Rain
Detail

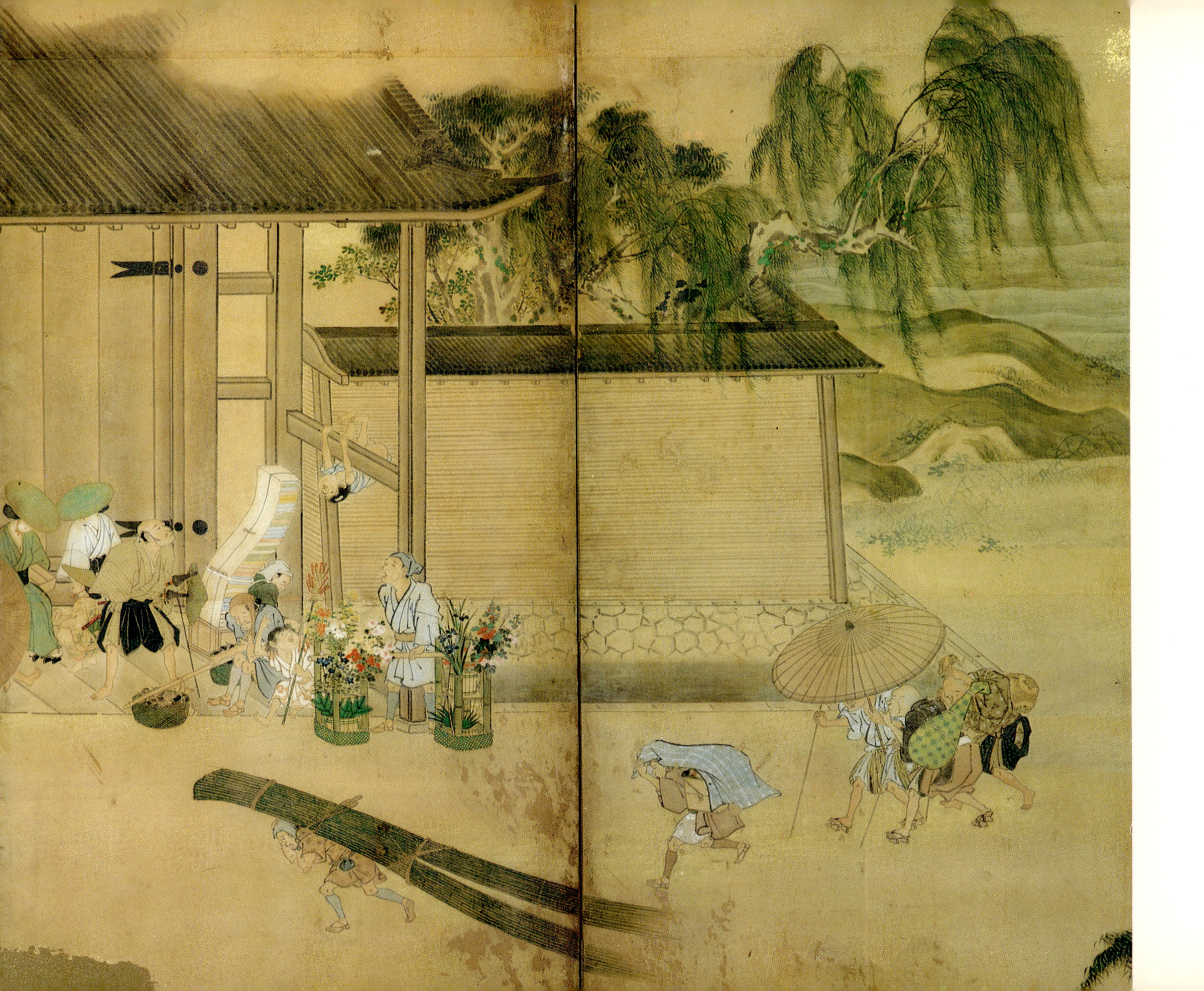

16.
TAKING SHELTER FROM THE RAIN
Edo period
by Kō Sūkoku (1737-1811)
Six-fold screen; ink and color on paper
163 cm. x 376 cm.
Seals: "Toryūō" and "Sūkoku"

Kō Sūkoku was a painter who followed the style of Hanabusa Itchō (1652-1724) and studied with a former pupil of Itchō, Sawaki Sūshi. While Itchō based his painting technique on that of the Kanō school, he developed a style that consolidated a number of features into a fresh, up-dated form of genre presentation. This screen is almost an exact copy of one with the same title by Itchō belonging to the Mary and Jackson Burke Collection, New York. The major difference between the Itchō original and the Sūkoku copy is the addition here of three more figures heading towards the gate in the fourth panel. This screen, nevertheless, exhibits the individuality of the artist, Sūkoku, in the clarity of the brushwork.

The scene depicted might have been one observed by the artist as a number of people of varying backgrounds are made temporary companions as they take shelter together from a sudden shower. The scene is set by the outer wall and gates of a large residence. The low-hanging clouds suggests only a brief, passing shower, but the agitation of the willows and bamboo enforces a stronger feeling. Among the people rushing toward the main gate are an itinerant priest and a man carrying a load of bamboo poles. A simple survey of the various types of people gathered under the eaves suggests the commercial and colorful nature of Japanese society during the Edo period. At the main gate are a flower vendor, a vegetable seller, lower class warriors, a nun, and performers of the lion mask dance. Huddled under the smaller gate at the left are a priest, children, a message courier, and a mother breast feeding her infant. The geniality of this scene, and its simple expression of a common humanity, are very touching.[13]

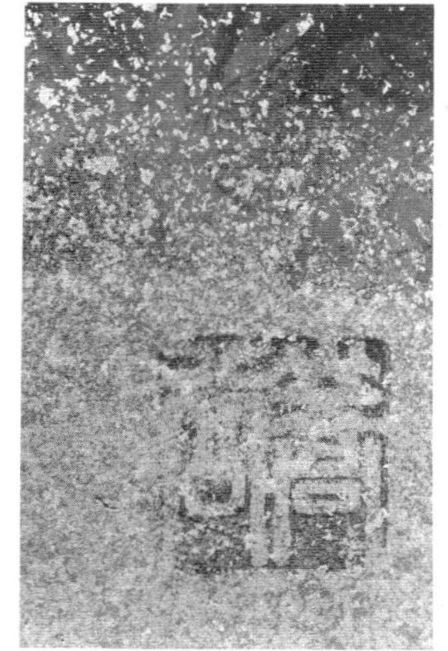

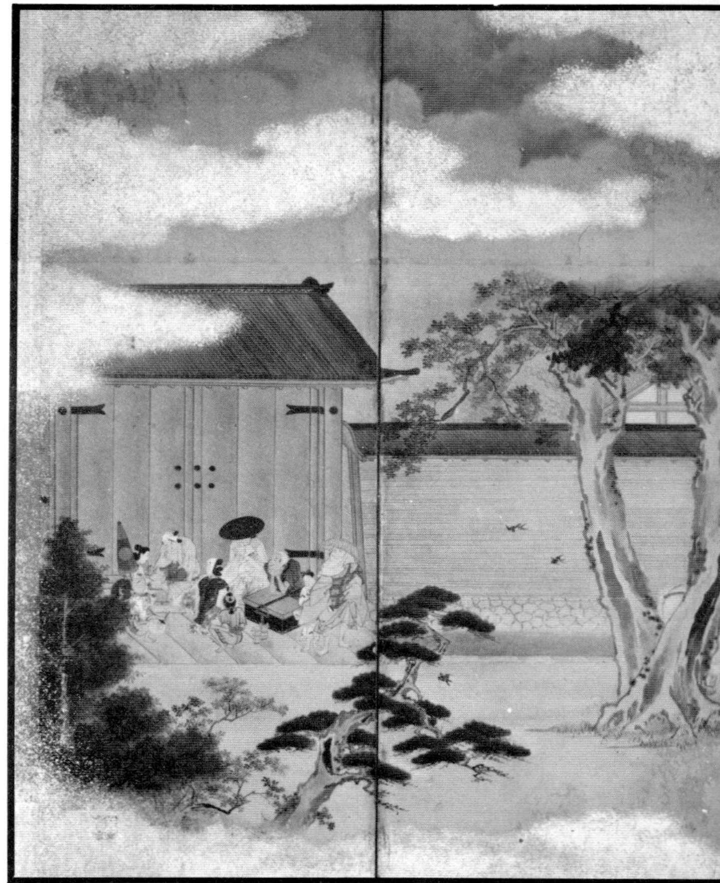

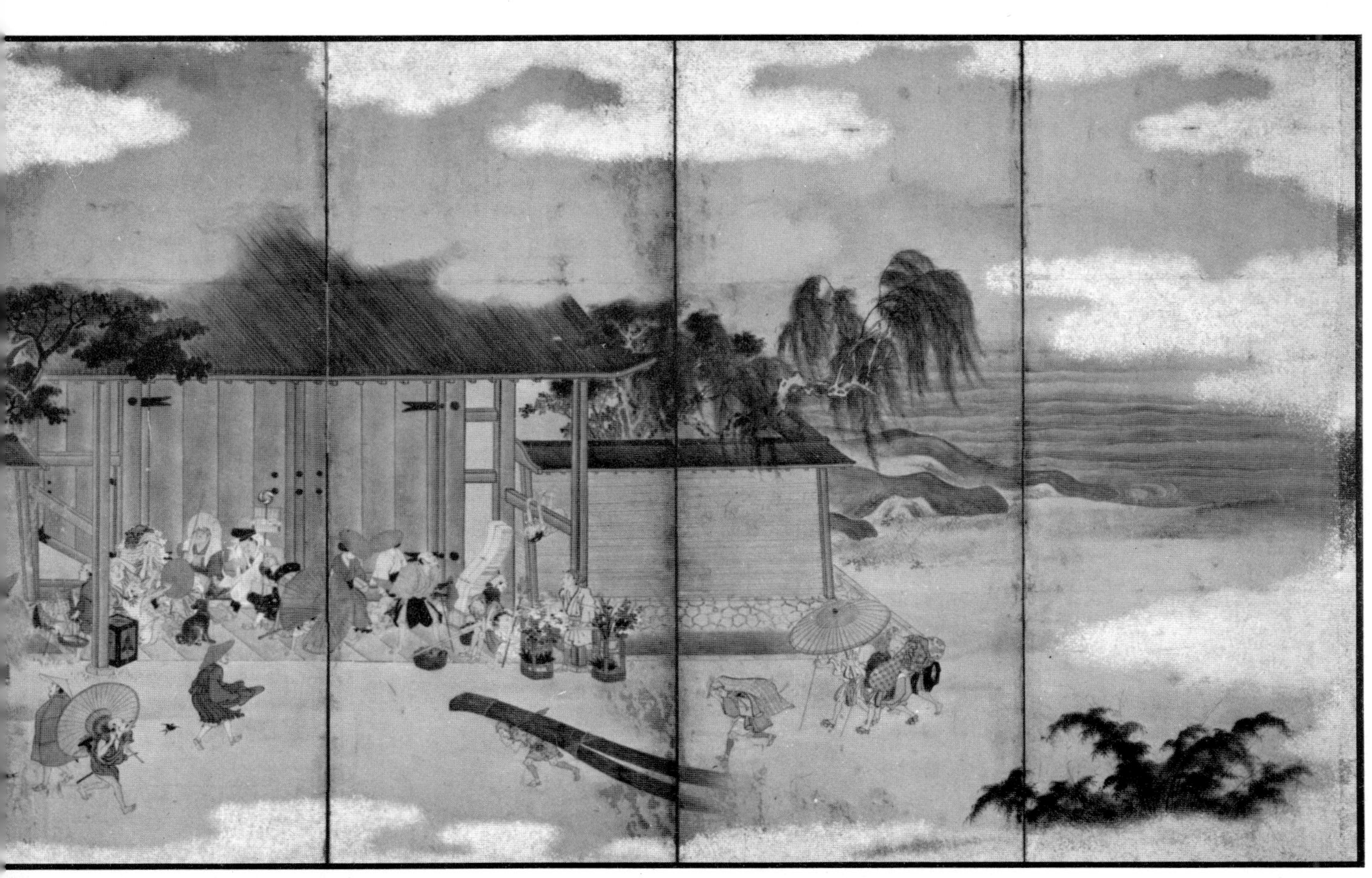

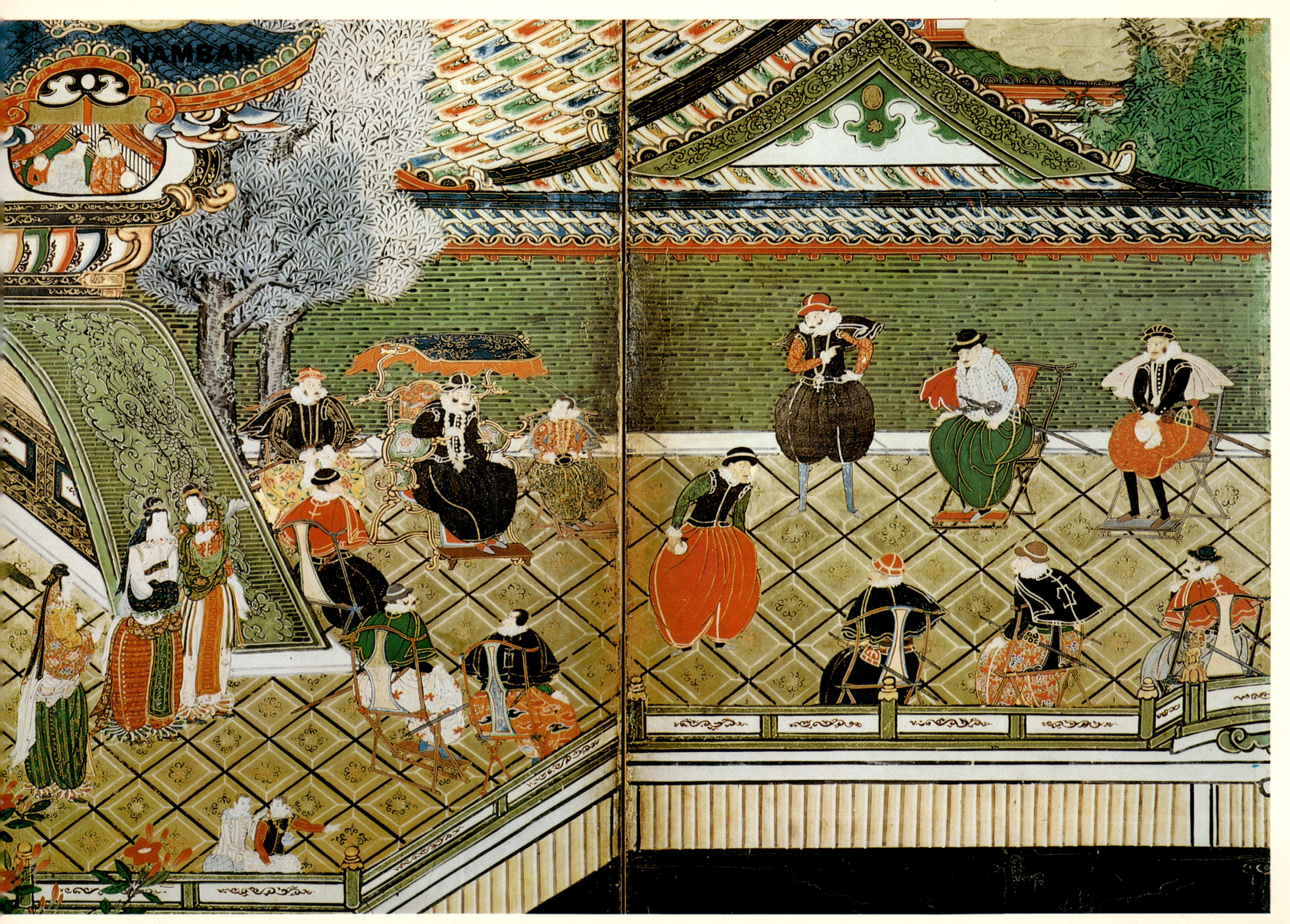

NAMBAN

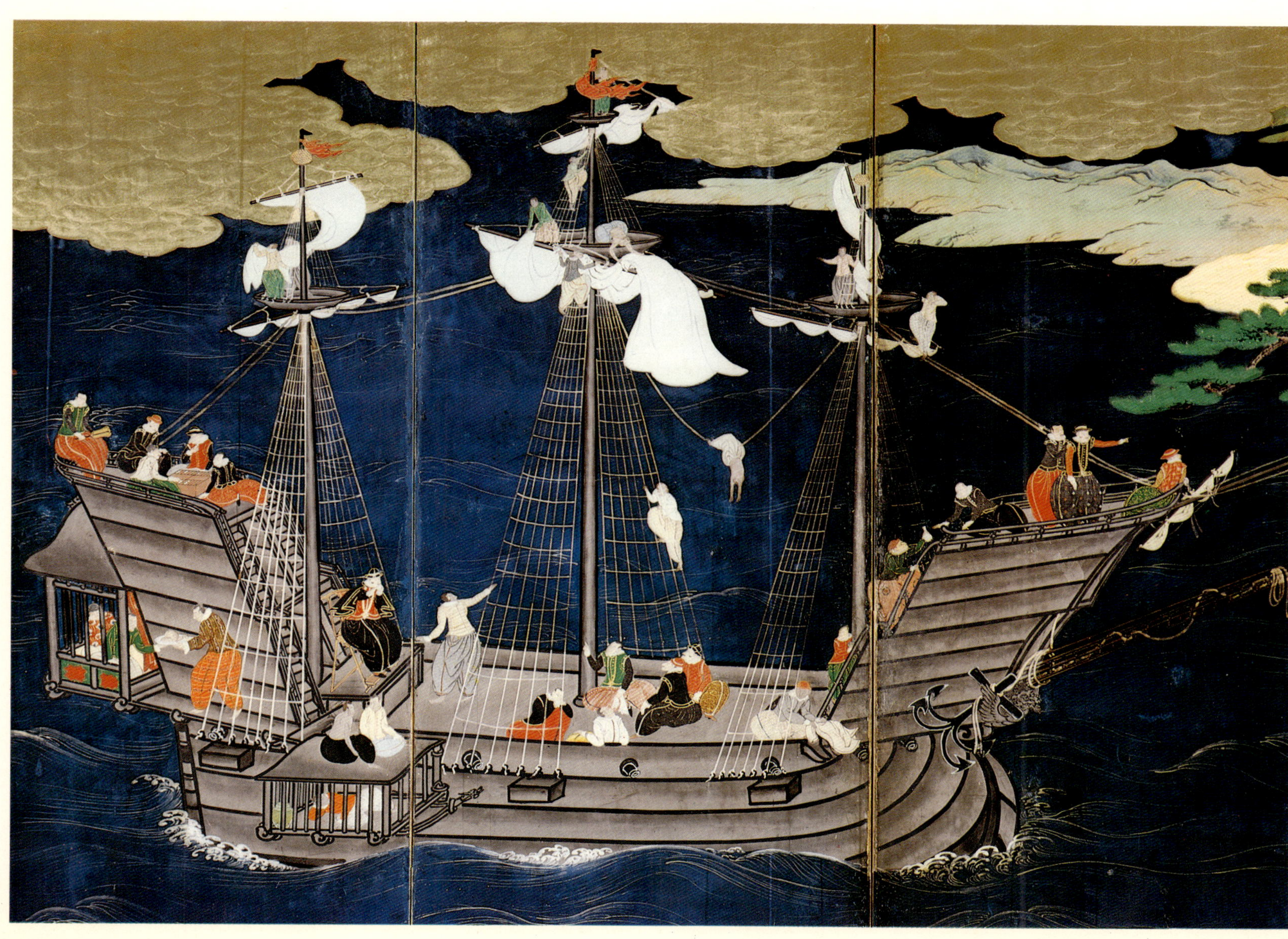

17.
Namban
Detail right screen

17.
NAMBAN (Southern Barbarians)
Momoyama period, seventeenth century
Pair of six-fold screens; color and gold on paper
182 cm. x 371 cm. each

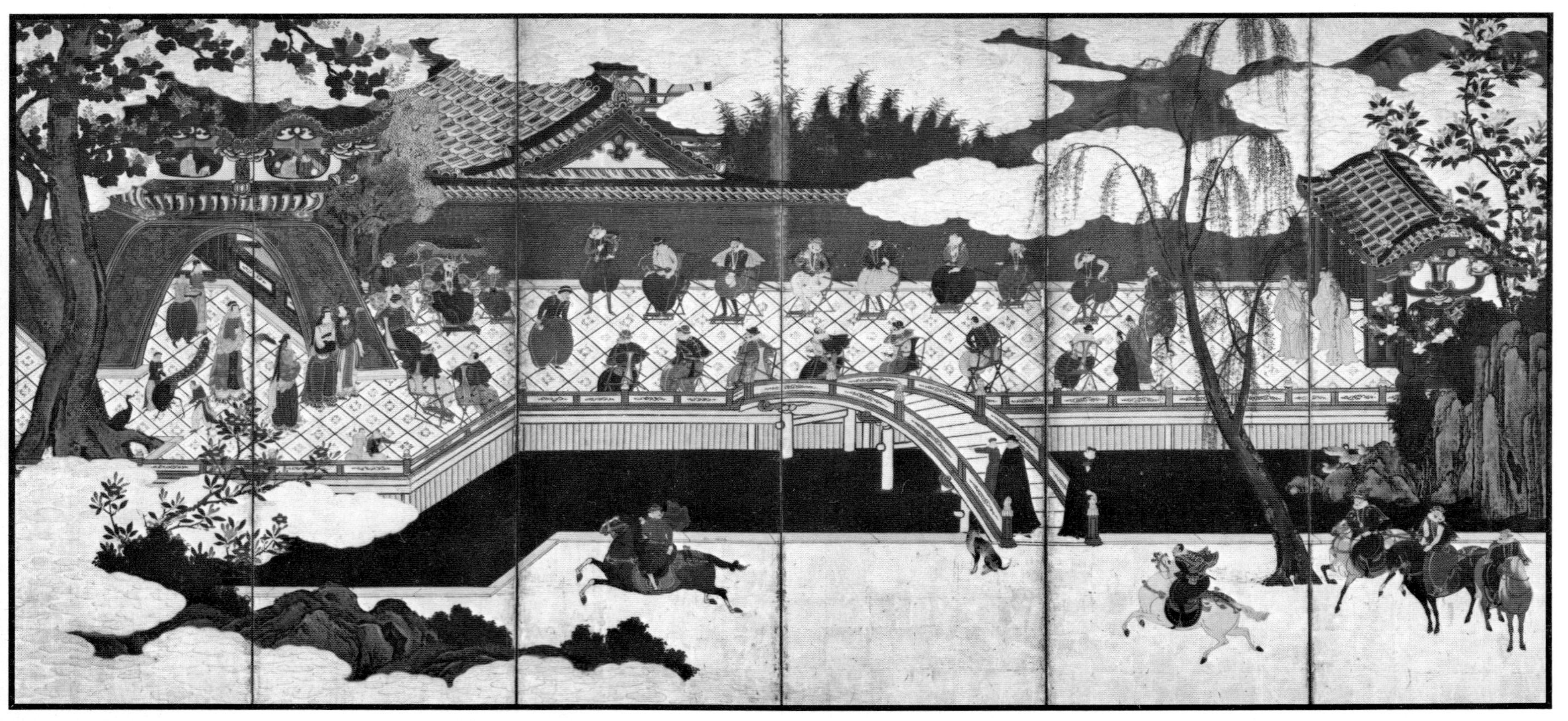

Initial contacts with Western culture in the middle of the sixteenth century opened the eyes of the Japanese to novel material goods, such as guns and crafts, and to new spiritual concepts. The customs and manners of the *nambanjin* (literally, "southern barbarians") who came to Japan were both curious and fascinating to the Japanese. Although the foreigners who arrived in the sixteenth century were primarily Portuguese merchants and Jesuit priests, they were given the designation "southern" simply because they came in boats from the south and entered Japan at harbors like Nagasaki and Sakai. The appearance of the Namban screen documents the degree of interest the Japanese took in these visitors from abroad.

Namban screens are very popular in Japan and the fifty or more that are extant are broadly divided into three categories:

1. pairs that show the ship docking in Japan on the left screen, and a procession of foreigners toward a church on the right screen
2. pairs showing the foreign ship leaving a foreign port on the left screen, and the same ship at anchor on the right screen
3. pairs with the depiction of a foreign land on the left screen, and the ship at dock on the right screen.

The Suntory Museum of Art's Namban screens are an excellent example of the third category. On the right screen the ship is at the dock and the sails are being furled. A party, including the captain of the ship and their missionary companions, have gone on shore with a load of goods for trade. Although the left screen is intended to be a depiction of a foreign country, Japanese artists were hampered by the paucity of available reference materials to assist them in their composition. For that reason, the clothing of the figures is only approximate, and the background looks as though the scene were set in China.

The preservation of this screen pair is excellent. It has been suggested that these screens may be the work of Kanō Sanraku (1559-1635). [14]

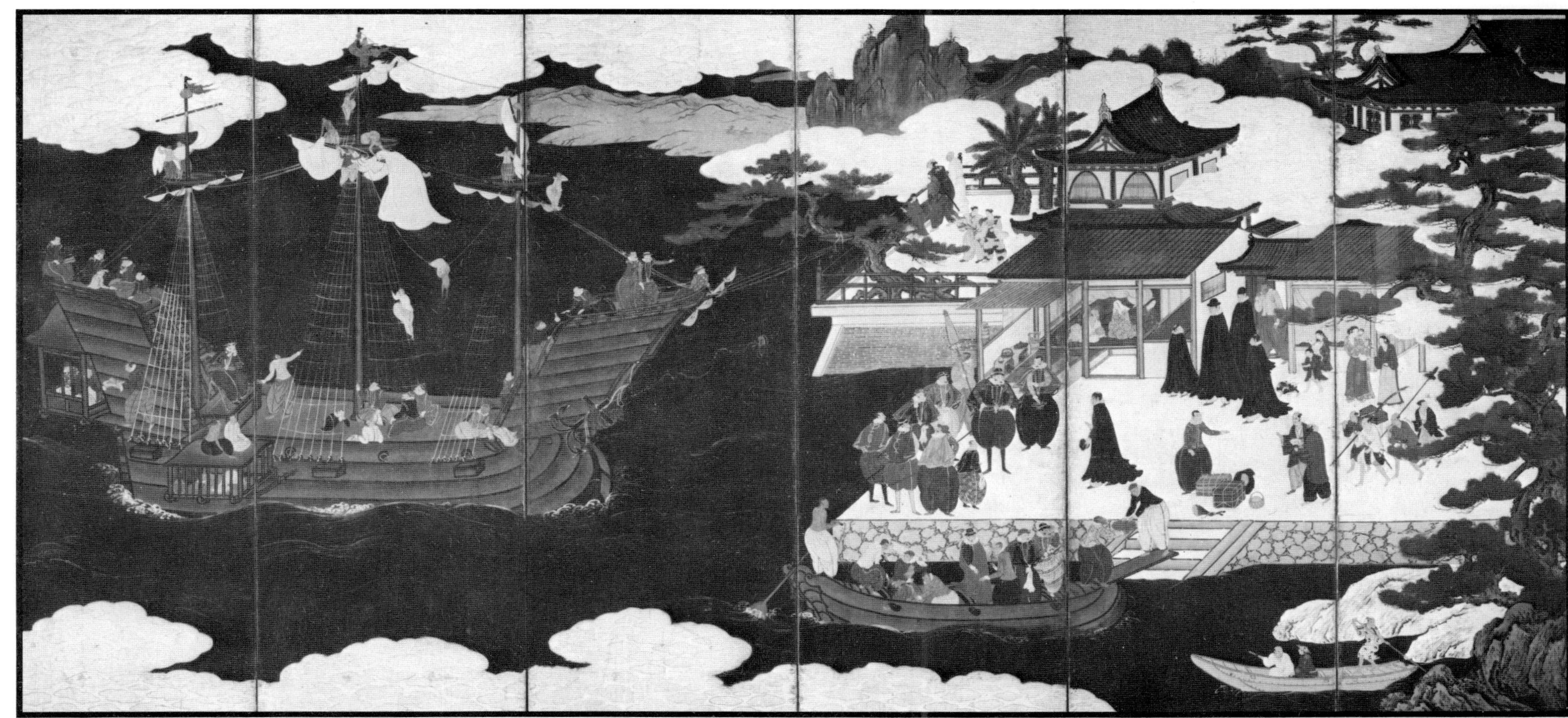

Notes and Reference Bibliography

The study of Japanese genre paintings of the sixteenth and seventeenth centuries is still a new field. A large exhibition of Rakuchū-Rakugai screens at the Kyoto National Museum, and the publication of that revised catalogue in 1966, clarified the historical development of one major category of genre painting. The other categories are not yet as thoroughly studied. The citations Professor Okada kindly wrote for this catalogue suggest a number of interesting features about the individual paintings in this exhibition. The brief notes that follow and the reference bibliography, which indicates where individual screens have been published, were compiled to assist those who wish to pursue an investigation of the subject. It is perhaps inevitable that, as translator, I have introduced distortions and misperceptions for which Professor Okada has my apologies. It has been a great pleasure to work with the Suntory Museum of Art on this exhibition.

Emily J. Sano

1. "Higashiyama and Kitano"
Published:
Takeda, Tsuneo, et al. *Yūraku–Tagasode: Nihon Byōbu-e Shūsei*, vol. 14. Tokyo, 1977: pp. 56-57.
Yamane, Yūzō. *Momoyama Genre Painting.* Translated by John M. Shields: Heibonsha Survey of Japanese Art, vol. 17. New York and Tokyo, 1973: fig. 148.
Kyoto National Museum, ed. *Rakuchū-Rakugai Zu.* Tokyo, 1966: No. 57.
For a discussion of the Chōen-ji screens, see Sakakibara, Satoru. *"Kyō Meisho Zu Byōbu"* (Screens of Celebrated Places in Kyoto). *Kobijutsu* 50 (February, 1976): pp. 30-32.

2. "Rakuchū-Rakugai"
Published:
Tsuji, Nobuo, ed. *Rakuchū-Rakugai Zu: Nihon no Bijutsu,* No. 121. Tokyo, 1976: pl. 79.
Kyoto National Museum, ed. *Rakuchū-Rakugai Zu.* Tokyo, 1966: No. 28.

3. "Celebrated Places in Ōmi Province"
Published:
Suwa, Haruo. *Shokoku Fūzoku-zu Byōbu.* Tokyo, 1977: pls. 47-52, text pp. 196-197.
(This publication by the Mainichi Newspaper introduces 23 genre screens that depict specific geographic locations. It consists of one bound volume of plates and text, and a separate folder of large, full screen color reproductions.)
For a discussion of the use of the *Shō-shō Hakkei* theme by Japanese painters of the Muromachi period, see Murase, Miyeko. "Two Views of the *Shō-shō Hakkei*", *Japanese Art.* New York, 1975: pp. 117-120.

4. "Sumida River"
Published:
Suwa, Haruo, ed. *Shokoku Fūzoku-zu Byōbu.* Tokyo, 1977: pls. 53-56, text pp. 198-199.
The *"Kinsei Shokunin Zukushi E-Kotoba"* has been published in a number of places. See Suzuki, Susumu. *"Kuwagata Keisai Hitsu Kinsei Shokunin Zukushi E-kotoba"* (A Handscroll Enumerating Modern Trades by Kuwagata Keisai). *Kobijitsu* 187. And Tamabayashi, Haruo. *"Kinsei Shokunin Zukushi E-Kotoba".* *Ukiyo-e Kai,* 3-1.

5. "Merrymaking under the Cherry Blossoms"
Published:
Yamane, Yūzō. *Momoyama Genre Painting.* Translated by John M. Shields: Heibonsha Survey of Japanese Art, vol. 17. New York and Tokyo, 1973: fig. 147.
Kyoto National Museum, ed. *Rakuchū-Rakugai Zu.* Tokyo, 1966: No. 61.

6. "Entertainments at a House of Pleasure"
Published:
Takeda, Tsuneo, et. al. *Yūraku–Tagasode: Nihon Byōbu-e Shūsei,* vol. 14. Tokyo, 1977: pl. 68.
Kaneko, Fusui, ed. *Nikuhitsu Ukiyo-e Shūsei.* Tokyo, 1977: pl. 31 (vol. I) and p. 183 (vol. II). (This lavishly illustrated two volume publication of the Mainichi Newspaper focuses on screens and hanging scrolls dating from the late Momoyama period and extending through the Edo period.)

7. "Tagasode"
Published:
Takeda, Tsuneo, et. al. *Yūraku–Tagasode: Nihon Byōbu-e Shūsei,* vol. 14. Tokyo, 1977: pls. 101-102.

8. "Okuni Kabuki"
A lengthy, but highly romantic account of the Okuni legend can be found in Kincaid, Zöe. *Kabuki.* Benjamin Blom, Inc., New York, 1965: pp. 49-57. (First edition: MacMillan & Co., 1925). An excellent survey of the major features of Okuni Kabuki is in Gunji, Matsukata. *Kabuki.* Translated by John Bester. Tokyo and Palo Alto, 1969: pp. 18-19.

9. "Flower Viewing at Ueno and a Kabuki Theatre"
Published:
Kobayashi, Tadashi. *"Den Hishikawa Moronobu Hitsu Kabuki Zu (Nakamura-za Naigai Zu) Byōbu ni Tsuite"* (Concerning screens of Kabuki scenes: Scenes inside and outside the Nakamura Theatre attributed to Hishikawa Moronobu). *Museum,* No. 8, 1977: p. 9.
A screen pair which bears the signature of Hishikawa Moronobu in the Freer Gallery, Washington, D.C., includes a composition also called "Flower Viewing at Ueno" which is identical to the left screen of the Suntory pair. For an illustration see Takeda, Tsuneo, et. al. *Yūraku–Tagasode: Nihon Byōbu-e Shūsei,* vol. 14. Tokyo, 1977: pl. 41.

10. "Archery Contest at Sanjūsangen-dō"
The inscription in the first panel is a record of a contest which reads as follows:
Among two hundred forty-five peaceful archers:
From 30 to more than 900 hits . . . . *129 men*
From 1000 to more than 1,900 hits . . . . *64 men*
From 2000 to more than 2,900 hits . . . . *23 men*
From 3000 to more than 3,900 hits . . . . *14 men*
From 4000 to more than 4,500 hits . . . . *6 men*
From 5000 to more than 5,900 hits . . . . *7 men*
From 6000 to more than 6,700 hits . . . . *3 men*
Over 7,500 hits . . . . *1 man*

11. "Horse Races at Kamo"
Published:
Kyoto National Museum, ed. *Rakuchū-Rakugai Zu.* Tokyo, 1966: No. 86.

12. "Fishing Scenes"
Although this pair of screens has not been published, other cultivation pictures may be studied. See Narazaki, Muneshige. *"Shiki Kōsaku Zu Byōbu"* (A Four Seasons Cultivation Picture Screen). *Kokka* 963, (1973). For examples of Chinese cultivation and weaving pictures, see: Umehara, Kaoru. *Sō Ōchō to Shin Bunka: Zusetsu Chūgoku no Rekishi,* vol. 5. Tokyo, 1977: pl. 150 (Freer Gallery, Washington, D.C.) pl. 152 (Nanking Museum, Nanking).

13. "Taking Shelter from the Rain"
Published:
Tsuji, Nobuo. *"Hanabusa Itchō Hitsu Amayadori Zu"* (Taking Shelter from the Rain by Hanabusa Itchō). *Kokka* 920, (1968): pp. 34-35.
For a discussion of the painting in the Burke collection in English, see Murase, Miyeko. "Taking Shelter from the Rain", *Japanese Art.* New York, 1975: pp. 292-295.

14. "Namban"
    Published:
    Sakamoto, Mitsuru. *Namban Byōbu: Nihon no Bijutsu,*
      No. 135. Tokyo, 1977: pls. 42-43.
    Doi, Tsugiyoshi. *Kanō Sanraku/Sansetsu: Nihon Bijutsu
      Kaiga Zenshū,* vol. 12. Tokyo, 1976: pl. 22, and p. 132.
    Yamane, Yūzō. *Momoyama Genre Painting.* Translated by
      John M. Shields: Heibonsha Survey of Japanese Art, vol.
      17. New York and Tokyo, 1973: fig. 154.
    Takamizawa, Takao. *"Shin Hakken no Kanō Sanraku Kei
      Namban Byōbu"* (A newly discovered Namban screen in
      the style of Kanō Sanraku). *Kobijutsu* 37 (June, 1972):
      pp. 98-100.
    Okamoto, Yoshitomo. *Namban Art of Japan.* Translated by
      Ronald K. Jones: *Nihon no Bijutsu,* vol. 19. Tokyo and
      New York, 1972: color pl. 13, fig. 15.
    Cooper, Michael S.J., ed. *The Southern Barbarians.* Tokyo
      and Palo Alto, 1971: figs. 1 and 101.
    Sakamoto, Mitsuru, et. al. *Namban Bijutsu to Yōfūga:
      Genshoku Nihon no Bijutsu,* vol. 25. Tokyo, 1970: color
      pls. 61-62.
    Okamoto, Yoshitomo. *Namban Byōbu.* Tokyo, 1970: pls.
      40-41, text pp. 137-139.
    Noma, Seiroku. *The Arts of Japan,* vol. 11. Translated and
      adapted by Glenn T. Webb. Palo Alto and Tokyo, 1967: pl.
      184.
    Narazaki, Muneshige. *Nikuhitsu Ukiyo-e,* vol. 1. Tokyo,
      1962, pls. 89-90.

Chronological Table

600	700	800	900	1000	1100	1200	1300	1400	1500	1600	1700	1800
552—645	645—794	794—1185				1185—1334		1334—1568		1568—1615	1615—1868	
Asuka Period	**Nara Period**	**Early Heian Period** 794—897	**Heian period**	**Late Heian Period** 897—1185		**Kamakura Period**		**Muromachi Period**		**Momoyama Period**	**Edo Period**	

Bibliography

Akiyama, Terukazu. *Japanese Painting.* Lausanne, 1961.

Grilli, Elise. *The Art of the Japanese Screen.* New York and Tokyo, 1970.

Kondō, Ichitarō. *Japanese Genre Painting: The Lively Art of Renaissance Japan.* Translated by Roy Andrew Miller. Rutland and Tokyo, 1961.

Kyoto National Museum, ed. *Rakuchū-Rakugai Zu.* Tokyo, 1966.

Murase, Miyeko. *Byōbu: Japanese Screens from New York Collections.* New York, 1971.

——————. *Japanese Art: Selections from the Mary and Jackson Burke Collection.* New York, 1975.

Noma, Seiroku. *The Arts of Japan,* vol. II. Translated and adapted by Glenn T. Webb. Palo Alto and Tokyo, 1967.

Okamoto, Yoshitomo. *Namban Art of Japan.* Translated by Ronald K. Jones: *Nihon no Bijutsu* 19. New York and Tokyo, 1972.

Takeda, Tsuneo, et al. *Yūraku—Tagasode: Nihon Byōbu-e Shusei,* vol. 14. Tokyo, 1977.

Yamane, Yūzō. *Momoyama Genre Painting.* Translated by John M. Shields: Heibonsha Survey of Japanese Art, vol. 17. New York and Tokyo, 1973.

Friends of Japan House Gallery

Mrs. Vincent Astor*
Mr. and Mrs. Douglas Auchincloss*
Mr. and Mrs. J. Paul Austin*
Mr. and Mrs. Armand P. Bartos*
Mr. Joe Brotherton*
Dr. and Mrs. Walter A. Compton*
Mrs. Cornelius Crane*
Mr. and Mrs. Edgar M. Cullman, Jr.
Mr. and Mrs. Lewis B. Cullman
Mr. and Mrs. Richard M. Danziger
Mr. and Mrs. C. Douglas Dillon*
Mr. and Mrs. Peter F. Drucker*
Mrs. Frederick L. Ehrman
Mrs. Richard Ellis
Mr. and Mrs. Myron S. Falk, Jr.*
Mr. and Mrs. Charles A. Greenfield*
Mr. Louis W. Hill, Jr.*
Mr. and Mrs. William H. Johnstone*
Ms. Margot P. Kneeland*
Mr. Yale Kneeland III*
Mrs. H. Irgens Larsen
Mrs. Louis V. Ledoux*
Mr. and Mrs. Henry A. Loeb*
Mr. and Mrs. Richard D. Lombard
Mr. and Mrs. Stanley J. Love*
Mr. and Mrs. C. Richard MacGrath
Edward John Noble Foundation
Mr. and Mrs. S. Morris Nomura*

Mr. and Mrs. Joe D. Price*
Mrs. John D. Rockefeller 3rd*
Mrs. Aye Simon*
Mr. and Mrs. Isaac Shapiro
Mr. Irwin M. Stelzer
The Florence Loucheim Stol Foundation
Mr. and Mrs. Donald B. Straus*
Miss Alice Tully
Mrs. Arnold L. van Ameringen*
Mr. Henry P. van Ameringen
Mrs. Lila Acheson Wallace*
Mr. Richard W. Weatherhead*
Ms. Lucia Woods*

*Founder